# SHIRE GARDEN HISTORY

# The English Rococo Garden

## Michael Symes

Printed in Great Britain by C. I. Thomas & Sons (Haverfordwest) Ltd, Press Buildings, Merlins Bridge, Haverfordwest, Dyfed SA61 1XF.

British Library Cataloguing in Publication Data: Symes, Michael. The English rococo garden. — (Shire garden history. V5). 1. Gardens: Landscape design. I. Title. 712.60942. ISBN 0-7478-0129-0.

*(Cover) The garden at Woodside, Old Windsor, Berkshire. Watercolour by Thomas Robins, c.1750. (Private collection. Photograph: Sotheby's.)* .

*(Title page) The Red House at Painswick, Gloucestershire.*

*(Below) View of the gardens at West Wycombe, Buckinghamshire, including the Temple of Venus. Engraving by William Woollett after William Hannan, 1757.*

# Contents

# Introduction

There are considerable difficulties in attempting to define the English rococo garden. The subject is beset by contradictions and confusions, and it might even be argued that the label serves no useful purpose. However, it has increasingly been applied to English gardens, particularly those of the mid eighteenth century, since the 1970s and it may therefore be helpful to look at the various strands that contribute to a sense of rococo. The publicity material of one or two gardens open to the public refers to rococo, and those who write on garden history have come to accept it as a term descriptive of a certain genre. The word is therefore used in practice, with an implicit expectation that it will convey something, and it is the intention of this book to work towards an understanding of what constitutes rococo in a garden.

In preparing this survey the author is conscious of the pioneering work of John and Eileen Harris, who together have put the rococo garden firmly on the map, by researching and publishing the work of Thomas Robins and Thomas Wright, which in turn drew attention to designers such as Richard Bateman and gardens such as Painswick in Gloucestershire. It is no exaggeration to say that the development of the idea of rococo has come from this work. The term itself was not used at the time with regard to English gardens and has been so applied only in modern times. Its use as an art historical category dates from the 1840s.

The word 'rococo' is familiar from the worlds of art and architecture and has been borrowed for gardens. It is most commonly understood in its application in Britain to interior decoration, particularly plasterwork, or to ceramics and other *objets d'art*. Painting and illustration (books and trade cards) also show a development of rococo style. The movement can be said to date from the late 1720s onwards, but painting and illustration precede decoration and objects. France was very much seen as the source of the movement.

The essentials of rococo are intricacy, scroll-like forms and shapes (C and S), elaborate ornamentation, asymmetry, and often a sense of lightness, playfulness and decoration for its own sake. It has been described as a 'feminine' style. Yet the word literally relates to *rocaille*, pebblework or rockwork, which immediately adds a further and specialised dimension, while the second half of 'rococo' comes from *coquille*, shell. It has to be admitted that in Britain the rococo movement generally, so strong in France and Germany, and extravagant in Italy and Spain, did not make great headway, and of the artists working in such areas as rococo silverware in Britain a good many came from the Continent, as the exhibition on English Rococo at the Victoria and

*River god and cascade deep within the grotto at Goldney, near Bristol, Avon. (Courtesy of Professor Robert Savage.)*

Albert Museum in 1984 showed. As regards formal architecture, Britain was virtually untouched by rococo, although its influence is sometimes seen in interior decoration. Some particularly fine examples of rococo plasterwork, for instance, can be found in houses of the period — Hagley (Worcestershire), Farnborough Hall (Warwickshire), Felbrigg (Norfolk), all of which had notable gardens. The finest British rococo craftsman was one whose field was furniture — Thomas Chippendale.

But if the flame of English rococo flickered intermittently and sometimes feebly in other arts, it burned brightly in the area of the garden. Garden artefacts were often ephemeral, rapidly constructed and relatively inexpensive, and experiments were possible on a scale which could not be contemplated when building a house. The extravagances and intricacy of rococo could find fitting shape not only in such artefacts but also in the design and layout of flower-beds and paths. Once one accepts the adoption of the word rococo for gardens, however, there is a danger that attempts will be made to read rococo into a number of eighteenth-century gardens that do not justify it, and unfortunately that has already happened. At one extreme 'Capability' Brown's massive parks have been described as rococo on the grounds that they use curves and serpentine lines (especially the lakes), but the scale of those parks is surely inconsistent with the innate smallness of rococo. Again, the eighteenth-century garden as a whole has been synonymised with rococo, and this is clearly unsatisfactory and meaningless.

In this book the idea of the rococo garden as being a question of approach, feeling or spirit, rather than a definable form, will be advanced and thus categories such as Gothic and chinoiserie will be discussed which are forms in their own right but which nevertheless can be described as rococo in certain cases. It is particularly a phenomenon of the mid century (concentrated in the years 1740-70), but there are elements which come from different periods and enter the story of the garden at different times. This leads to some problems, such as the facts that serpentine paths in garden wildernesses are known in the late seventeenth and early eighteenth centuries, some way ahead of the movement proper, and grottoes such as Alexander Pope's (from 1719) displayed *rocaille* features which on one hand were in advance of their time in the purely rococo sense but on the other hand had a lengthy ancestry in the form of decorated French and Italian grottoes from much earlier, and indeed from as far back as antiquity. There are also freaks such as the island in a lake at Wanstead House, Essex, cut in the shape of the British Isles, which dates from before 1736. The time scale is therefore ragged, and the differing aspects of rococo cannot be unified in one neat whole.

It is important to distinguish between rococo gardens, which are small in scale and very scarce today, and rococo elements within a large garden, which are more numerous since a large garden is much more likely to have survived than a small one. Further, it will have been more visited and recorded by visitors, so that our knowledge about large gardens, whether they survive or not, is much greater.

In architecture, rococo is thought of as the final phase of the baroque, a lightening of solidity and heaviness, replacing grandeur with elegance.

In gardens, on the contrary, rococo may be seen as an expression of something new, a freedom of style and a sense of experiment that link it to the freeing of the English garden from centuries of formality. In its fantasy and imagination it looks forward rather than back and can be seen to have affinities with 'romantic' Gothic which led to the Gothic novel and, in other spheres, to the romantic movement itself.

Other relevant forms of rococo which may have had some influence on gardens are porcelain, to be discussed in the chapter on garden sculpture, and painting. Jean Antoine Watteau was actively painting from 1704 and his Arcadian world was one which could readily be translated into garden design. Many of his works displayed figures pursuing pleasure in a setting of a garden, park or landscape, and they were often engraved for circulation in Britain. English painters and engravers of gardens followed suit in peopling their scenes. After Watteau came François Boucher and then Jean Honoré Fragonard, who, progressively from 1750, evolved an ornate rococo approach to his depiction of gods, goddesses and contemporary figures. Again these were often set against backgrounds of gardens; and garden sculpture, plinths and other artefacts in the paintings draw them close to the world of real gardens.

One possible area of confusion must be cleared up, and this is that the term rococo has been used in Europe for a garden concept of a different kind. In Germany, in the middle years of the eighteenth century, gardens changed from baroque to so-called rococo before the English landscape style made its appearance in that country: the essence was a series of small elaborate garden rooms or compartments in a basically formal plan, sometimes with Chinese-style buildings and also mock ruins. Thus, at Veitshochheim in Bavaria, an apparently formal garden had contrasting compartments, dark and open areas, and chinoiserie in both buildings and sculptures. In total there were about three hundred sculptures of varying kinds, many amusing, and an astonishing array of garden furniture. These enclosed compartments are not to be found in the English rococo garden. The ornate trellis-work of the German gardens could be seen also in France, where a movement designated rococo flourished in gardens between 1727 and 1755, characterised by intimacy, enclosure and *treillage*, again with oriental pavilions. Only in the use of curving paths, chinoiserie and asymmetry did such gardens have anything in common with England. Indeed, it is sometimes claimed that rococo is basically an un-English concept, and that is why European expressions of it so often failed to take root in England. One factor is that rococo was regarded as a French style, and there was much general suspicion of the French, their religion and their absolutist monarchy, quite apart from the actual hostilities of the Seven Years' War.

Unlike in Europe, rococo was not confined to the princely few. Indeed rococo gardens by virtue of their small scale are much more likely to have been owned by the middle class, perhaps merchants or *nouveaux riches* who had a modest home and a few acres but nothing on the scale of an aristocratic family seat such as Blenheim or Castle Howard. For example, Benjamin Hyett at Painswick was from a family of lawyers and Francis Yerbury of Belcombe Court, Wiltshire, was a clothmaker. Rather than an aristocratic game, English garden rococo can be seen as a new imaginative expression of the artist/owner, taking delight in trying out ways in which to adorn a small space.

Rococo was also often the province of the amateur. The owner would frequently be his own designer and, even if he had recourse to advisers such as Thomas Wright or Sanderson Miller, they would not be professional consultants in the same sense as their contemporary 'Capability' Brown, even though they might be paid for their contributions.

Francis Coventry, in an essay in *The World* (12th April 1753), ridiculed the excesses of rococo, but his shafts were aimed more at the upstart owners who fancied they had taste but lacked it than at rococo itself: his Squire Mushroom created gardens 'which contain every thing in less than two acres of ground. At your first entrance, the eye is saluted with a yellow serpentine river, stagnating through a beautiful valley, which extends near twenty yards in length. Over the river is thrown a bridge, *partly in the Chinese manner*, and a little ship, with sails spread and streamers flying, floats in the midst of it.' A small grove winds in and out, covering the same ground continually, and you are then led to a hermitage of tree roots. You are taken to 'a pompous, clumsy and gilded building, said to be a temple, and consecrated to Venus; for no other reason which I could learn, but because the squire riots here sometimes in vulgar love with a couple of orange-wenches, taken from the purlieus of the play-house.' Yet, if handled imaginatively, rococo features could have great charm and appeal.

It is not possible to come to an exact definition of our subject. This book sets out to explore rococo themes in the English garden and to stimulate further thought, debate and investigation. Research is by no means exhausted, and it is to be hoped that new information or the rediscovery of actual gardens will still be forthcoming.

My thanks go to a number of garden historians who have helped in discussion and the provision of material, notably Mavis Collier, John Harris, Andrew Skelton and Nigel Temple. Lord Dickinson has been most helpful in providing information and material on Painswick.

# Rocks and shells

The word 'rococo', as we have already seen, is cognate with *rocaille*, which embraces rockwork or pebblework. The movement started in France as early as the sixteenth century, with stones, rocks and shells being used for the purpose of decorating grottoes and fountains in gardens, and those who worked in this field were known as *rocailleurs*. The term *rocaille* then became applied to an ornamental style that was used first in the decorative arts and then in other arts more generally, again starting in France at the beginning of the eighteenth century. Its characteristic, which leads the style to what we recognise as rococo, is the convolution of line into curves and scroll shapes, with a sense of lightness and fanciful experiment.

Grottoes have a long and distinguished ancestry that stretches back to the mythological caves of antiquity. In both France and Italy in the Renaissance and later there were wonderful structures, some of which were adorned with elaborate patterns of shells and stones. Sometimes these grottoes would represent mysterious allegorical worlds, as at Boboli and Castello. These two were naturalistic in interior appearance, representing caves and contrasting with the more obviously room-like grottoes at, say, Villa d'Este or Isola Bella. Common to both types is the presence of water, in pools or fountains, on occasion in the form of practical jokes to drench the unwary visitor. These elements of cave or room and type of decoration were all inherited by English grottoes.

In England the grotto was introduced in the seventeenth century, via the room built into the house at Woburn Abbey, Bedfordshire (*c.*1627), the water grotto at Wilton, Wiltshire (1630s) and through John Evelyn, whose tunnel at Albury, Surrey, was modelled on the 'Pausilippo' in Italy where Virgil was said to be buried. All three were heavily Italianate. The subsequent development of the grotto through the eighteenth century tells us a good deal about the development of the landscape garden and also relates directly to the rise of rococo. The grottoes in the first half of the century were formal in structure, although their decoration could be highly 'natural' and irregular. The early grottoes could look — as they did in France or Italy — like classical pavilions or temples from the outside (for example William Kent's classically façaded grotto at Esher Place, Surrey, or that of Salomon de Caus at Wilton) while the interior would often be basically of regular construction, for example the concept of a main chamber and apsidal side chambers at Stowe, Buckinghamshire, or Stourhead, Wiltshire, both from the 1740s. But the decoration was another matter. With reference to his grotto at Twickenham, Middlesex, Alexander Pope announced, 'Approach — Great Nature studiously behold!', where the nature to be beheld consisted of rocks, stones and other geological specimens sent to Pope by friends who had toured widely through Britain and Europe. Thus there was petrified rock from Wookey Hole, Somerset, and volcanic lava from Vesuvius. Pope boasted that everything on the walls of his grotto was in its pristine, natural state, not having suffered polishing or chiselling into shape. He worked on the grotto from *c.*1720 to his death in 1744, adding to it continually. To the question, 'Was it rococo?' the answer must be no, since the decoration was natural and not the highly artificial result of rococo planning, although art may have had a hand in the placing and layout of the natural objects. Nonetheless, it pointed the way towards the use of stones, rocks and pebbles for decorative purposes which became more mannered in some of the great grottoes later in the century.

The grotto at Goldney, near Bristol, Avon, on the other hand, does show distinctive rococo features. Begun in 1737 (though the decoration was not completed till 1764), it is of its time in its construction of a principal chamber with columns, as might be found in France or Italy, but ahead of its time in the decoration, which included precious stones, tufa, burnt slag and shells. Amethysts, quartz, jasper, agate and other minerals compete with coral and shells for our attention. Pope's grotto was something of a geological display, but with Goldney the balance tips from geology to decoration, although there are fascinating geological examples. But what catches the eye is their effect and their placing for colour and design. Goldney therefore faces in both directions, to the past and to the future.

At the same period there was great interest in constructing patterns from pebbles. Pebbles were an obvious way of surfacing the floor of a grotto (Stourhead) and could be patterned to a greater or lesser degree. In one sense they were the natural choice of flooring since they were 'natural' to the world of the grotto. But they could also form patterns on walls, and the most famous example, which is in a good state of repair, is the Pebble Alcove at Stowe by William Kent, where the Cobham arms are picked out in coloured pebbles.

The grotto at Stourhead (1748) struggles to transcend its regularity of structure. As at Goldney, there are signs of forward movement. The exterior is faced with what is popularly known as tufa (a pitted limestone rock) though it should properly be called spongestone or honeycomb rock. This substance, used as a facing on a brick core, became very popular in the second half of the century for creating rococo effects with grottoes and other smaller constructions. Appearance apart, there is considerable significance in the Stourhead grotto in its positioning on the circuit, in its role in the Aenean symbolism of much of the garden, and in its function of looking out across the water back to Stourton church, as if to bring the visitor back from pagan to Christian. The

Decoration of the interior of the grotto at Goldney, near Bristol, Avon. (Courtesy of Professor Robert Savage.)

*Rockwork cascade and view of gardens, West Wycombe, Buckinghamshire. Engraving by William Woollett after William Hannan, 1757.*

figures in white lead — the River God and the Sleeping Nymph — by John Cheere have a meaning in the symbolic context but are in any case linked to rococo by their form and texture.

Rockwork was by no means confined to grottoes. There is a rockwork arch at Stourhead and a rock tunnel at Studley Royal, North Yorkshire. A rockwork cascade featured at West Wycombe, Buckinghamshire, in the 1750s but was subsequently modified. William Woollett's engraving depicts a fine example of rococo work — natural boulders creating a striking effect and related to art by the figures of the sleeping nymphs at the sides. The River God presides, as at Stourhead. At Belton, Lincolnshire, there was an equally impressive cascade of similar style, incorporating a ruined chapel, and there was another at Marino, near Dublin.

Rocks were generally imported into gardens for their various effects, though in some cases the existing stone was exploited, most spectacularly at Hawkstone, Shropshire. In Piercefield (or Persfield) near Chepstow, Gwent, the natural rock was hollowed out into a small cave to form a grotto decorated with the usual minerals and into a large one called the Giant's Cave. Over the entrance crouched a stone giant, brandishing a great rock threateningly. In course of time the rock dropped from his grasp and he himself later fell down the cliff.

Tufa decoration was sometimes used as dressing on buildings which were not grottoes. Richard Woods, a landscape designer of the late eighteenth century, used it commonly to decorate small classical and other buildings. It was also used on Fisher's Hall (1750) at Hackfall, North Yorkshire.

In the second half of the century grottoes became more natural in appearance, both inside and out. Some were adapted to meet the changing fashion: for example, Lord Lincoln's grotto at Oatlands, Surrey, started in the 1760s very much as a garden building, with three rooms on the lower floor and one large chamber on the upper floor, with regular windows. But during the 1770s it was substantially altered, particularly with regard to the decoration within, with the result that a variety of designs was to be seen. The large upper chamber was decorated with a bustling mixture of shells, rocks, ammonites, spar and quartz, while each of the lower rooms had its own distinctive design. One room was a bath room, another a chamber with coloured zigzag stripes, and the

*Chamber in grotto, Oatlands, Surrey. (Courtesy of the Architectural Review.)*

third a glittering cave of blue crystal spar, complete with stalactites. The flooring of the ramp circling up to the upper chamber was peppered with trotter bones and cows' and horses' teeth.

The masons responsible for the reworking of Oatlands in the rococo style were the Lanes, father and son, of Tisbury, Wiltshire. It is possible that Joseph Lane, the father, worked at Stourhead; he certainly created the startling grotto at Painshill, Surrey, in the 1760s and was then joined by his son Josiah for the Oatlands project. Josiah then set up on his own account and built grottoes at Bowden Park, Bowood, Fonthill and Wardour (all in Wiltshire), and possibly at St Anne's Hill, Surrey, in the 1790s, which had sparwork similar to that at Oatlands and Painshill. The Lanes' two great innovations were the naturalising of the exterior of the grotto to make it appear to be a cave rather than a piece of man-made architecture, and the use of spar and other crystals to produce a fantasy interior of sparkle and glitter, also naturalistic in appearance.

The Lanes' grottoes sacrificed meaning and solemnity of purpose to decoration for its own sake. Earlier grottoes such as those at Stowe and Stourhead have a definite meaning in their classical and mythological associations, while one would have approached, say, Pope's grotto with a sense of reverence, although an exception was his enemy, Lady Mary Wortley Montagu, who wrote of the God of Dullness being installed in the cave. Later grottoes certainly had a function in the landscape and provided a point of focus and interest in the scene, sometimes spectacularly so, but the earlier symbolism was lacking. Painshill grotto, one of the finest in the land, was dazzling in its main chamber of spar, 40 feet (12 metres) across, and in its elaborate water effects but was a wonder *per se* rather than for any broader function it served. Charles Hamilton, the owner of Painshill, was essentially a 'visual' man and created his gardens with an infinite variety of scenes and vistas, and the grotto was to be seen as an extraordinary visual display. The whole of the grotto island was dotted about with strange outcrops and clumps of tufa, giving the impression that it all belonged to some exotic marine location.

At Bowood and Wardour Josiah Lane experimented with a more 'primitive' effect. The grotto at Wardour is simple and cyclopean in the way boulders were piled together to create in-and-out chambers in a crude undecorated form. Charles Hamilton, late of Painshill but since 1773 living in retirement in Bath, devised the grotto at Bowood as part of a whole rockwork complex that has been described as 'a rococo valley'. Josiah Lane executed Hamilton's plans, which had been drawn up *c*.1781 for the Earl of Shelburne. The centrepiece was a waterfall, supposedly modelled on the falls at Tivoli as depicted by Gaspard Dughet (Poussin), behind which wove a warren of passages from which the visitor could look out through a curtain of falling water. On each side of the stream which stretches from the cascade was a grotto-type tunnel, now much dilapidated. Further up the hill, some way back from the waterfall, is a Hermit's Cell, again rudely fashioned in rock, with ammonites in the ceiling.

Fonthill had two grottoes, as well as several tufa constructions which spring up here and there, reminiscent of the tufa-studded island at Painshill. An earlier grotto was by the older Lane *c*.1760. Much remains although there has been considerable decay. Parts of the grottoes were known as the Hermit's Cell and the Hermit's Cave, and one of the free-standing tufa works was intended to represent an ancient cromlech, thereby giving an air of apparent historicity.

Ascot Place, Berkshire, has a grotto dating from the late eighteenth century that combines the 'natural' rocky exterior appearance of Wardour with some of the interior detail and design of Oatlands and Painshill. It was designed by the owner Daniel Agace, and the mason was Turnbull, a Scot. A lakeside grotto, it has two main chambers leading off into smaller tunnels and niches. The larger chamber has a pool in the floor, as at Painshill, and the ceiling is a mass of feldspar-covered stalactites. The zigzag pattern of Oatlands is repeated in a sparkling brown mineral. J. C. Loudon considered that its only rival was Painshill, and it is, along with Goldney, the most superb surviving grotto.

A grotto dating from *c*.1750 at Wimborne St Giles, Dorset, had a flint-faced front leading to one room decorated with minerals and a second with shells, which are sprayed around in disordered plenty, no attempt apparently having been made to impose any pattern or design on them.

Shells were used more and more to decorate grottoes, the task often being undertaken by the ladies of the house. It was a laborious and painstaking business — Goldney grotto, for example, took over 25 years to complete. In this case the craftsman, Mr Warwell, used over 200,000 English shells, and a good many from the East and West Indies and West Africa, borne home in Thomas Goldney's ships. The shells, numbering over two hundred species, were often arranged in patterns to give three-dimensional effects or to simulate, for example, a ram's head. There are swags of shells which have 'a wonderfully rococo exuberance', as Professor Robert Savage, the expert on Goldney grotto, describes it. The Duchess of Newcastle decorated the upper room of the grotto at Oatlands with shells, and in some instances one could find a complete shell room rather than a grotto, as at Goodwood, West Sussex, where the Duke of Richmond's wife and daughters spent considerable time creating an enchanting display of colour, shape and patterning. A stunning shell room was designed for the loggia of the east pavilion at Mereworth Castle, Kent, where the cornice and ceiling

*Engraving of the now lost shell temples, Stowe, Buckinghamshire.*

design was picked out in shells with motifs of birds and flowers. On the walls shells were arranged to represent dolphins of various sizes. This astonishing enterprise was attributed to an invalid woman.

The queen of shellwork was undoubtedly Mary Delany (1700-80). She worked mainly in Ireland, which with its profusion of native shells gave special impetus to this art form. She started at Killala, County Mayo, where, rising at 7 o'clock in the morning, she would ornament the walls and roof with shells which the Bishop of Killala had collected, some from abroad. So many shells were plundered from Irish beaches that it was feared they would run out: in 1788 Lord Donegall had £10,000 worth that he had not yet unpacked. Perhaps the best shell house of all was that created in 1752-4 by Lady Tyrone at Curraghmore, County Waterford, where shells jostle with crystals and pearls to feast the eye.

Just as tufa could be used for buildings other than grottoes, so shells could be found away from grottoes or shell rooms. Pope had a shell temple in his garden at Twickenham — an openwork arbour with shells applied on the columns — which fell down, and there were a pair of shell temples at Stowe in the form of rotundas.

Although extreme artifice is normally present and visible in rococo, its spirit can be sensed equally in what might be termed 'fanciful naturalness', which would include the elaborate structures at Bowood and Painshill where part of the intention was that they should look natural. If Bowood waterfall stood by itself it would not be markedly rococo: but taken as part of a complex which includes the grotto, the passages and the Hermit's Cell, the whole valley takes on a rococo feeling.

*Underside of grotto bridge, Painshill, Surrey, in process of restoration. (Courtesy of the Painshill Park Trust.)*

# Garden sculpture

Although some elements of rococo are discernible in patterns of planting or shape of water (see next chapter), its manifestation in gardens is mainly through artefacts. Buildings and other structures, and the way in which they were decorated, were the most obvious media through which the rococo spirit could be expressed. But there is one other artefact that can be equally eloquent, although surprisingly little attention has been paid to it by garden historians, and that is sculpture.

Sculpture has played an important role in gardens since classical times. The Romans used to display statuary as much in their gardens as indoors, sometimes to such an extent that the garden became an open-air sculpture gallery. It was also a tribute to the gods, goddesses, emperors and heroes of the day. In the Renaissance Italian villa gardens revived the practice, with schemes assuming elaborate dimensions and meanings. Such a garden as Boboli, Florence, had well over a hundred pieces, and the most famous sculptors of the time were employed, such as Donatello, Giambologna and Michelangelo. Often the pattern of sculpture would have some allegorical or interpretable meaning, although that of the monster-filled garden of Bomarzo remains a subject for debate. Sculpture would normally be used to emphasise formal elements of the design of gardens — a group in a fountain at the intersection of avenues, or rows of figures lining an *allée* — and could be simply decorative rather than carrying a significance.

The practice spread from Italy to France, where, again, complex programmes of sculpture could be found. At Versailles the allegory of the figures depicted in a massive scheme bore unmistakable reference to the king and thereby served as an iconographical tribute to, and enhancer of, his glory. In Britain the use of statuary was less strongly marked, although the larger gardens such as Nonsuch, Surrey, or Hampton Court, Middlesex, contained figures that, in the same tradition as in France, referred to the monarch. At Nonsuch there was a Fountain of Diana which was emblematic of Queen Elizabeth I in both her chastity and her role as mother of her people.

Such sculpture in formal gardens was generally of marble or other stone, although the use of bronze was well known from classical times and often found in Britain in the seventeenth century. But the heyday of sculpture in British gardens, which can be dated to the period from *c*.1680 to *c*.1780, stems largely from the introduction of casting in lead, a process which came in from the Low Countries. The use of lead had two important results: first, it lent itself to a particularly attractive finish and could take coloured paint, although classical marble statues were treated with gesso and then painted; second, a number of figures could be cast from the same mould, so that, although it hardly amounted to mass production, nonetheless a leadworker could offer a range of stock figures as well as special custom-designed pieces. This encouraged the spread of the use of garden sculpture.

The first half-century of the heyday corresponds with much continuing formality in garden design, so the work of the two masters in that period, John Van Nost and Andrew Carpenter, was and is mostly to be found in gardens that were still largely formed on geometrical lines. There are splendid collections of figures at Powis Castle (Powys), Melbourne Hall (Derbyshire), St Pauls Walden Bury (Hertfordshire) and Studley Royal (North Yorkshire). But as the eighteenth century progressed there was a tendency to use sculpture more naturalistically in accordance with the transition to more natural-looking gardens, and the figures themselves changed from predominantly classical or Renaissance — heroes, classical deities, easily recognised figures of legend — to rustic and contemporary. Because lead statues could be painted,

*Lead figures: (left) drummer-boy attributed to John Cheere, c.1760; (right) shepherd with bagpipes at Powis Castle by Andrew Carpenter or John Van Nost, c.1710.*

*Bacchus, Clifton Hampden, Oxfordshire. Lead figure repainted in original colours.*

and usually were, figures could be made lifelike far more effectively than with marble.

Even in the early figures of Van Nost and Carpenter there is a reaching out towards the lyrical and ornate that anticipates some of the later, more obviously rococo work. In the catalogues of both men there is a predictable emphasis on the classical, but it is not always classical of an heroic kind. Both sculptors (who shared moulds, Carpenter having been assistant to Van Nost) advertised rural classical figures: Pan, satyrs, shepherds and shepherdesses. Thus the figures on the second terrace at Powis Castle, Welshpool, which could be by either Van Nost or Carpenter, are four most delightful Arcadian figures, two shepherds and two shepherdesses, accompanied by dogs or lambs. The bagpipes played by one of the figures were known to have been used in classical times.

At Rousham, Oxfordshire, Van Nost's figures of a faun and Pan in Venus's Vale contribute strongly to the 'feel' of the area, a rural retreat fit (as Horace Walpole said) for a Roman emperor. The treatment of the scene in landscape terms is wooded and sylvan, very different from the formality of spread-out parterres or neatly trimmed groves, so the figures are integrated into the scenery in a new way, although sculpture had been placed in the gardens of Caserta, Italy, for topographical effect.

Melbourne Hall has a collection of exquisite pieces by Van Nost (unfortunately depleted by theft in 1989), ranging from a series of four quarrelling pairs of *amorini* to the kneeling figures of a blackamoor and an Indian on the lawn, carrying vases above their heads. These two figures in particular, which may represent Africa and India, were widely copied during the century, perhaps from the same moulds. There is no doubt that they were painted, the white garments contrasting with the black bodies. Such decoration shows a foreshadowing of rococo even at this early date (1700-10). It was not always a question of colour, for the Powis shepherds and shepherdesses bear traces of having been painted to look like stone. It was recommended at the time that all lead sculpture should be given some sort of weather protection either with paint or with an oil finish.

The painting of leadwork to make it appear like stone or marble is very much part of the eighteenth-century approach to gardens, the creation of illusion. So often we find that things are not what they appear to be, whether it is a matter of perspective that deceives, the shape of a piece of water that appears to alter when viewed from different points, or artefacts that have a deliberately misleading effect. Not only was leadwork painted but buildings were commonly made of wood or brick and then given a render to make them appear to be of stone.

Lead figures were being painted from the late seventeenth or early eighteenth centuries and anticipate rococo in another medium, porcelain, where figures which could sometimes be miniature versions of garden figures did not appear in Europe until *c*.1730. But once porcelain had taken hold, the influence may then have swung round so that garden statuary followed what was happening in porcelain. It is not until the mid century that we find the full flowering of the rococo garden figure. Van Nost and Carpenter had gone, but their moulds survived and were taken over by John Cheere, who maintained production of classical lead figures which were both from well established models and of his own making. For instance, he made the Sleeping Nymph in white lead for Henry Hoare's grotto at Stourhead, Wiltshire, and likewise the River God there. But Cheere's yard contained a much wider selection of sculpture from which to choose, as J. T. Smith in *The Streets of London* reveals: 'The figures were cast in lead as large as life, and frequently painted with an intention to resemble nature. They consisted of Punch, Harlequin, Columbine, and other pantomimical characters; mowers whetting their scythes; haymakers resting on their rakes; game-keepers in the act of shooting, and *Roman* soldiers with *firelocks.*'

This list contains a number of items that do not appear in the Van Nost and Carpenter catalogues but which have direct parallels in rococo porcelain in the *commedia dell'arte* figures of Punch and Harlequin, such as were produced by many of the porcelain factories in Europe, notably by Bustelli at Nymphenburg and by Kändler at Meissen. Such figures were also being made in England, particularly at Bow and Chelsea.

Another fashion, as indicated in Smith's list above, was the creation of rural workers, such as gardeners with scythes or other implements. At Wrest Park, Bedfordshire, in the early eighteenth century, Van Nost and Carpenter supplied a large number of figures including not only a Neptune with trident but a gardener with a rake. This was early on, but later products became even more naturalistic. A gardener leans on his spade in a very realistic pose at Burton Agnes, Humberside, while the 'Green Man of Peele' (Somerset), a completely painted figure of a sportsman aiming his long gun, may be identifiable with the Cheere figure of a gamekeeper in the act of shooting. Certainly the Cheere model was to be found in Scotland at Blair Castle, Tayside, in the 1750s, and likewise at Biel House, Cambridgeshire. From gardeners and farmworkers it was a natural progression to portray animals such as the lead cow at Biel. This is contemporary with Horace Walpole's introduction of specially coloured sheep (real, not lead) in his garden at Strawberry Hill, Middlesex, for their effect in the view.

Another strand was the portrayal of everyday life and occupations. A pair of figures by or after John Cheere demonstrates this approach — an orange-seller and a drummer-boy. These figures too have their equivalents in porcelain, for the Capodimonte works in Italy, for instance, in addition to *commedia dell' arte* characters, produced several contemporary figures — cakesellers, tradespeople and such like. The naturalism of garden statues was satirised by Richard Cumberland in 1785, who wrote of visiting a certain Sir Theodore Thimble. Finding a well dressed gentleman with a hat under his arm, in an attitude of politeness and civility, Cumberland assumed this must be Sir Theodore and removed his own hat ... 'but, how was I surprised to find, in place of Sir Theodore, a leaden statue on a pair of scates, painted in a blue and gold coat, with a red waistcoat.' But 1785 is right at the end of the era of leadwork, which was shortly to be supplanted by Coade stone as a means of producing statues and also by a change in taste from rococo anyway.

Garden sculpture inevitably bears a relation to sculpture generally, and Louis François Roubiliac, one of the leading sculptors of the day, is often credited with introducing a rococo style to British sculpture. Some of his work did appear in gardens, such as his figures of Milton and Handel in Vauxhall Gardens, London, while his statue of Shakespeare, designed for David Garrick, was displayed in the temple on Garrick's lawn at his villa in Hampton, Middlesex.

Restoration of garden statuary, especially where it was painted originally, can present great problems. Sometimes there will be traces of paint to indicate the colour, but this might date from a period later than the original. Descriptions of colour are usually lacking in contemporary visitors' accounts of gardens, but it would be wrong to assume that the 'natural' lead colour of so much garden sculpture as we see it today necessarily gives us a good idea of what the figures looked like at the time. A fine example of a repainted statue is the Bacchus in the orchard at Clifton Hampden, Oxfordshire. Here the restoration is in what are claimed to be the original colours — auburn hair, pink flesh, purple grapes — which produce an altogether startling effect today although it would have been accepted as common practice in the age of rococo.

# Flower-beds and wavy lines

Flower-beds could play an active part in making a garden rococo, both in the outline shape of the bed and in the patterns in which flowers and low-growing shrubs were planted within it. The richest period for flower bedding was the Victorian era, when carpet bedding and related practices produced a great variety of elaborate patterns, yet the eighteenth century was by no means devoid of such interest. In the past it has sometimes been assumed that flowers were banished altogether at that time, in an age when 'Capability' Brown's lawns swept up to the walls of the house and swept away everything in their path too. However, continuing evidence has come to light of the cultivation of flower-beds, which in some instances have a close bearing on rococo.

Richard Bateman (1705-75) was one of the unsung innovators of eighteenth-century gardens. Thanks to John Harris's researches on Thomas Robins (see next chapter), we now know more about Bateman's garden at Old Windsor, Berkshire, and about his role in garden history. He inherited land in Essex from his wealthy father, who died in 1718, but moved to the Thames valley, where he leased a house near Old Windsor church which he called Grove House. He worked on his gardens from c.1730 and it is now clear that in two respects he was outstandingly ahead of his time. He introduced chinoiserie into gardens at an appreciably earlier date than its era of popularity; and he made telling use of flower-beds. Horace Walpole described Grove House as the kingdom of flowers. There were two flower gardens, one slightly earlier than the other. The earlier, before 1740, is depicted in a painting which shows a circular flower-bed in a confined garden area containing trees, a small pavilion, seats and a swing; although the shape of the bed is regular, the feeling of the whole scene is informal. The second, after 1740, was more noticeably asymmetrical with a haphazard disposition of flower-beds and pots around a seat on a low mount.

Walpole himself may have been influenced by Bateman in the matter of flowers, for when he established his Gothic house at Strawberry Hill, Middlesex, he sought to embellish the grounds with copious colourful plantings. It was not a large garden, but Walpole varied it with lawns, meadows, terraces, shrubs, flowers and trees, taking advantage of the views down to and across the Thames. We have seen that he even had some Turkish sheep and two cows which were expressly chosen for their markings to colour the view. An exuberant spirit informed Walpole's idea of his garden: it was to be 'nothing but *riant*, and the gaiety of nature'. The main feature was a spacious lawn, bordered by a serpentine wood of 'all kinds of trees and flowering shrubs and flowers'. Lilacs, acacias, honeysuckles, tulips, jonquils and syringas abounded — Walpole said he could load wagons with them. Interestingly, for someone who later disparaged chinoiserie when he found it elsewhere, Walpole created a small walled garden with a circular pool that he called Po-Yang and he even had Richard Bentley design for him a Chinese pavilion (unexecuted).

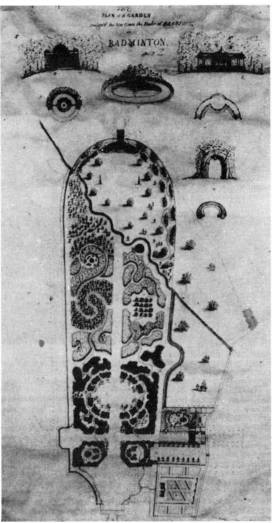

*Thomas Wright's plan for a flower garden at Badminton, Avon, 1750. (Courtesy of His Grace the Duke of Beaufort.)*

Whether or not we see the garden as in some sense complementary to the extraordinary fantasy Gothic of his house, the key to Walpole's garden is the 'gaiety of nature', not to be confined in formal walks, and thus in tune with the rococo spirit. The date is right too, for Walpole purchased his estate in 1748 and began work on the gardens immediately, adding to the initial area until he eventually had 46 acres (19 ha).

At the heart of the rococo period Thomas Wright was constructing a number of flower-beds, some of which were symmetrical and geometrical (he was a mathematician) but others were consciously asymmetrical — and very elaborate. His plan for a garden at Badminton, Avon, which unfortunately was never executed, is the essence of rococo in its scroll shapes, its lack of ordered balance, its intricacy, its divisions and its decoration by arches and buildings. We shall return to Wright in the next chapter.

Joseph Spence (1699-1768) was another whose flower-garden designs ranged from the formal to the informal. Working on a small scale, he planned the use of flowers in beds and containers for the houses of (usually) non-aristocratic owners who did not have the acreage to indulge in Brown-type expansive lawns and parks. Spence advocated the use of wild flowers, especially among groves and bordering walks away from the house. The use of colourful shrubs and flowers in areas well away from the parterres, where they would normally be expected to be found, was taken further by Philip Southcote at Woburn Farm, Surrey, and Charles Hamilton at Painshill, Surrey, where colour would punctuate the circuit walk in a very informal way.

There are many records of Southcote's *ferme ornée* at Woburn Farm (started 1735), which indicate the extensive and significant use of flowers and shrubs without regularity. There was a broad perimeter walk, much of which was bordered by a thick hedgerow in which were intertwined woodbine, jasmine and other flowering and scented creepers. At ground level the walk was lined intermittently by beds of flowers, shrubs and trees. Spence analysed in detail the plantings at one particular point in the walk. A 2 foot 6 inch (76 cm) wide border of flowers and shrubs contained three rows of progressively larger plants, starting with a front row including crocus and pinks, then carnations, lavender and so on in the middle, and hollyhocks, sunflowers and others at the back. Behind this border was a plantation of shrubs and trees, again with the lowest in front and the tallest at the back, for example holly and broom at the front, lilac and honeysuckle and others in the middle and large trees at the back, including beech, alder, hazel and hornbeam.

Such tiering was also used by Hamilton at his 'amphitheatre' at Painshill, where a flat lawn was encircled by shrubs and trees graded according to height. Painshill was noted for its shrubberies, one of which was adjacent to the house but others of which were scattered through the grounds, for example below the Gothic Temple, on the grotto island and in front of the Temple of Bacchus. The exact design of these shrubberies is not known, but from visitors' accounts they seem to have been informal. They were certainly colourful, and the effect, especially at the Temple of Bacchus, was cheerful — or *riant*, as Walpole would have said.

Other gardens made use of flowers and shrubs in different ways. William Kent, who is supposed to have been persuaded by Southcote to resume the planting of flowers in a natural way, underplanted flowering shrubs among trees at both Rousham, Oxfordshire, and Esher Place, Surrey. At the latter the grotto was 'overhung to a vast height with woodbines, lilacs and laburnums', as Walpole described it. The natural colour of the flowers was used to add to the effect of the building just as Hamilton was to do at the Temple of Bacchus.

The most intriguing use of flower-beds in the eighteenth century is at Nuneham Courtenay, Oxfordshire. Here William Mason, author of a long didactic poem, 'The English Garden', designed *c.*1770 an enclosed flower garden for Lord Nuneham, son of the first Earl of Harcourt, before he succeeded to the earldom and the estate. Lord Nuneham was much influenced by Jean Jacques Rousseau, who stayed at Nuneham Courtenay and is said to have sown many foreign wild flowers there. The flower garden embodies a concept central to Rousseau's thoughts of the simple natural life. This concept was that flowers should serve a moral purpose, that they should uplift as well as give pleasure. Following the natural approach, all straight lines were excluded from the garden, although the irregularity was carefully contrived by Mason, who based his design on a description in Book IV of 'The English Garden'. The overall shape of the garden in his plan is rather like a heart, with plantings serpentising their way along the edge. Within the garden is a lawn studded with beds, each of which has an irregular shape. They gave rise to the term 'kidney beds', although they are not all kidney-shaped. Some individual trees were planted in the lawn, and a number of busts and buildings commemorated philosophers, friends and appropriate classical deities such as Flora and Hebe. If the flowers on their own did not achieve their purpose of leading to virtue, there were inscriptions to make sure the visitor got the point. Mason's idea was that gardens should be created with the imagination of a poet and the eye of a painter. The beds were edged with a low bordering plant, presumably box, to pick out their irregular undulating shape, and the pattern of planting was often to place a tree or taller shrub in the centre and surround it with flowers or shrubs, often of a wild kind. Cultivated and wild flowers were mixed to demonstrate freedom and naturalness.

*Flower garden at Nuneham Courtenay, Oxfordshire. Engraving by William Watts after Paul Sandby, 1777.*

Two views of the garden in the 1770s, painted by Paul Sandby and engraved by William Watts, are reproduced here. The flower-beds would appear to be rococo in their shape, intricacy, lack of symmetry and making a lot out of a small space. However, this raises an interesting question. It may well be that Mason, consciously or unconsciously, took his shapes from rococo, since rococo was well established by 1770, but his and Lord Nuneham's motivation could not be further removed. For while rococo is essentially light and pleasure-seeking, sometimes even frivolous, the flower garden at Nuneham Courtenay had its serious moral role, although that was not intended to exclude delight.

The serpentine line is a prominent design feature of eighteenth-century gardens, but it is by no means restricted to mid-century rococo work. It affects the shaping both of paths and of water but can cause historical confusion since serpentine lines appear long before William Hogarth popularised the concept of the wavy 'line of beauty' in the 1750s, though his undulations are much more gentle. In general it can be seen as a reaction against straight lines in gardens, and some wonderfully convoluted forms were evolved. John Harris has drawn attention to the proliferation of wiggling lines in garden designs before 1730, including patterns in books by Stephen Switzer and Batty Langley, who coined

*Flower garden at Nuneham Courtenay, Oxfordshire. Engraving by William Watts after Paul Sandby, 1777.*

the term 'artinatural'. There may possibly be French antecedents, but the sheer scale of the movement in England makes it a recognisably English phenomenon. It has to be admitted that many of these early designs prefigure rococo and might indeed be identified with it. To preserve rococo for the mid-century period, one might need to classify these wavy-line designs as a genre of their own.

Paths, or walks, are a subject deserving of study in their own right. It has been mentioned that seventeenth-century 'wildernesses' (which were in fact tightly controlled and rather tame) often had winding paths. One such wilderness (*c*.1671) has been restored at Ham House, Surrey. By the early eighteenth century the fashion had definitely taken hold. Castle Howard, North Yorkshire, had a parterre in front with intricate paths winding in and out in between thick hedges; there is some doubt as to whether it was executed in this form, but the design exists. Further away from the house there was a wood on a hill, Wray Wood, which had mazy paths, possibly designed by Stephen Switzer. In Switzer's *Iconographia Rustica* (1718) there are several designs for serpentine paths within gardens that otherwise retain much geometry.

From that time paths wriggled about freely, sometimes in small town gardens and sometimes on large estates. Alexander Pope's 5 acre (2 ha) garden at Twickenham, Middlesex, had a wilderness and a few winding paths; so much was crammed into the limited space — amphitheatre, bowling green, wilderness, hothouse, vineyard, kitchen garden, grotto, obelisk, urns, cypress walk, shell temple — that one has to ask whether this garden, which dates from 1719 to 1744, can be described as rococo. As with his grotto, the answer is probably no, since, although some of the elements of rococo might appear to be present, the feeling — as at Nuneham — is altogether different. Just as the grotto had solemnity, so the ultimate point of the design of Pope's garden was reverential: the climax was the cypress walk that led up to the obelisk that commemorated his much loved mother.

In *The Clandestine Marriage*, completed by David Garrick and George Coleman in 1765, there is some good-humoured fun at the expense of Mr Sterling's anxiety to keep up to date with gardening taste. Garrick wrote the garden scenes, in one of which Mr Sterling asks his visitor Lord Ogleby what he thinks of the close walks:

*Lord Ogleby.*  A most excellent serpentine! It forms a perfect maze, and winds like a true lovers' knot.
*Sterling.*  Ay — here's none of your strait lines here — but all taste — zig-zag — crinkum-crankum — in and out — right and left — to and again — twisting and turning like a worm, my lord!
*Lord Ogleby.*  Admirably laid out indeed, Mr Sterling! one can hardly see an inch beyond one's nose any where in these walks. — You are a most excellent oeconomist of your land, and make a little go a great way.

The serpentising of water features seems to have occurred equally early. There is a plan of Moor Park, Surrey, from the 1690s, which shows a stream wiggling about, admittedly just outside the main garden. By the 1730s the practice was well under way — William Kent's serpentine rill at Rousham is a famous example. The Serpentine in Kensington Gardens, London, was created by Charles Bridgeman, working for Queen Caroline, by joining two streams in 1731, and the very name signifies recognition of the concept. Walpole said of Kent that, among his innovations, 'The gentle stream was taught to serpentise seemingly at its pleasure.'

The wavy line of both paths and water was taken up in a rococo context, and, as we shall see, the paths at Painswick, Gloucestershire, and the water at Wroxton, Oxfordshire, demonstrate this. It fits in well with rococo design and thinking and shows (as with grotto decoration) that established ideas could be absorbed and then given a new kind of life in their rococo embodiment.

# Thomas Robins and Thomas Wright

Thomas Robins and Thomas Wright, the first an artist, the second a designer, encapsulate what is most manifestly and identifiably rococo in the English garden. The work of Thomas Robins was brought to the forefront in the 1970s by John Harris: there was an exhibition of Robins's drawings and watercolours at the Heinz Gallery of the Royal Institute of British Architects in 1975-6, and this was followed by a two-volume edition of his works. At the same time Eileen Harris was working on the subject of Thomas Wright and his architectural designs, and this resulted in an edition of Wright's two suites, *Arbours and Grottos*, originally published in 1755 and 1758, with an introduction spanning his considerable garden involvements.

Thomas Robins (the Elder, 1716-70) came originally from Cheltenham although he settled later in Bath. Many of his drawings and paintings were concerned with that area, although he also illustrated gardens further afield. He toured various parts of Shropshire, Warwickshire, Dorset and the Thames Valley, producing views of the gardens for the owners, usually by means of watercolour on vellum. Not only did he depict gardens of the rococo period in his work from 1747 to 1766 but he gave a good many of the views the rococo borders which make his art so distinctive. So we have, as a result, a rococo artist depicting rococo scenes, in a unique and fascinating series. The borders are a study in themselves, ranging from birds, butterflies and feathers to leaves, tendrils, fruit, flowers and shells. Often there is a predominant motif within the border.

The most enchanting of Robins's views are the two of Woodside, Old Windsor, Berkshire. Acquired by Hugh Hamersley on his marriage in 1752, Woodside had a small garden, but full of delightful features. Illustrated on page 37 is the Orangery, itself a building with distinctly rococo tendencies such as the fretwork-style design of the windows and the whimsical use of birds on the roof. A trailing plant or creeper decorates the columns and curves above the windows of the Orangery almost as Robins borders his paintings with flowers. On each side of the Orangery are beds where there is a profusion of flowers and plants randomly mixed. Other shrubby beds are dotted around. As if to reflect the nature of these flowers, creepers and shrubs, Robins frames the picture with long tendrils which arch and interweave with leafy stems and flowers including periwinkles and orange-blossom. Dr Martyn Rix has identified the botanical and other natural history elements of Robins's borders, and his identifications are used in this book.

Another view is that shown on the front cover. The centrepiece is a Chinese bell-pavilion with an open fretwork screen on each side: this is

*Honington Hall gardens, Warwickshire. Watercolour by Thomas Robins, 1759. (Courtesy of the Sutton Place Foundation.)*

definitely a case of chinoiserie that is also rococo. There is some regularity in the lines of saplings that border the central area of lawn, but otherwise it is informal, with the paths serpentising off to the left, and flower-beds and seats arranged asymmetrically. Once more there is a Robins border of tendrils with leaves and flowers on stems that weave around them. Sweet pea, pink, honeysuckle, nasturtium and gold-laced polyanthus are depicted. Several aspects of gardening at the time are displayed in the painting: roller, rake, besom and scythe. It is not known who designed the garden at Woodside, but Thomas Wright would be a candidate.

Pan's Lodge, near Painswick, Gloucestershire, is one of the set of five views which Robins painted for Benjamin Hyett of Painswick, a garden to be discussed in the final chapter. Here the border is dominated by birds — barn owls, a nest of fledglings, a blackbird, a magpie and a kestrel. Instead of flowers, more 'woody' material is depicted — acorns, oak leaves, berries and nuts. A red squirrel completes the sylvan nature of the border. Pan's Lodge itself exhibits one remarkable piece of wriggling (just right of centre) and a fanciful gathering of Pan and his followers in the bottom right-hand corner.

Honington Hall, Warwickshire, was painted in August 1759. The garden is the work of that other master of the rococo, Sanderson Miller, who will feature in a later chapter. In this view there is a good deal of the kind of rococo scene that Miller devised at Wroxton, Oxfordshire, although, unfortunately, little survives. Another Chinese bell-pavilion, though very simple compared to that at Woodside, a winding lake, a temple, a rockwork grotto, a cascade and a chinoiserie bridge appear within a relatively small area. The plantings are totally irregular. The view was a record of Miller's recently completed layout for the owner, Joseph Townsend. The border has the character of the Woodside borders with tendrils, sprays of leaves and flowers, including cyclamen, jasmine, iris, ipomoea, tuberose, polyanthus, roses and pelargonium, as well as a colourful butterfly.

Thomas Wright (1711-86) was a mathematician and astronomer who formulated a theory about the Milky Way which was published in 1750 and which gained him fame. From that time onward, however, his garden interests took the upper hand, and he designed buildings or layouts for more than thirty gardens. He was particularly concerned to develop flower gardens close to the house. His principal patron and employer was Elizabeth, Duchess of Beaufort, and it was at Badminton, Avon, that much of his work was carried out over a considerable period of time. We have already seen his unexecuted plan for a flower garden, but fortunately a good number of his other designs not only came to fruition but have survived. In no sense can the huge estate of Badminton, with its endless grand avenues, be described as rococo, but Wright designed some quirky, eccentric buildings to put into the landscape. There was Castle Barn, a practical farm building but adorned with castellations, which inspired a number of similar barns on the estate. There was also Ragged Castle, constructed of stones of uneven sizes, now heavily overgrown, and the Hermit's Cell, a primitive rustic building of a kind that Wright specialised in. A thatched building of timber, it is dressed on the outside with roots and branches, while the interior has columns and arches with a knobbly wood effect. All the furniture is of wood, as is the loaf of bread on the table.

A large number of Wright's drawings exists — 175 in the Avery Architectural Library, Columbia University, New York, and more than 75 sketches and planting designs in a private collection in London. In the Avery collection are six plans and elevations for garden temples which look as if they were intended for a third volume, companion to those on arbours and grottoes. Wright's drawings cover a range of styles of building, classical, Chinese and Gothic, but he keeps returning to rustic, and this is his most characteristic and distinctive contribution to garden architecture. Thus, he draws a Gothic temple which has branches applied to its outside surface, and some open arbours or *tempietti* (little temples) where the columns are wreathed in climbing plants, and

*The ruins at Shugborough, Staffordshire, by Thomas Wright.*

tufts of growth are to be seen on the conical roofs.

In keeping with his mathematical interests Wright designed a number of geometrical rosaries, or flower-bed gardens. Using a compass, he drew tangential or intersecting circles to create great intricacy of patterning, as for example for Beckett Park, Berkshire, 1754-60.

One of Wright's most extensive commissions was at Shugborough, Staffordshire. In addition to work on the house in 1748-9 Wright was responsible for the serpentine canal, some chinoiserie, some Gothic buildings and the ruins which face the rear of the house across the Victorian parterre. These ruins have been modified since Wright's time, and the figure seen in the photograph is of Coade stone, which dates from later in the century. Contemporary paintings show a classical arcade opposite the ruins, across the water, and clearly this area was intended to bring together a configuration of classical elements just as Wright's Chinese bridge (now replaced) matched the Chinese House built by Thomas Anson. Another feature, which survives, is the Shepherd's Monument bearing an inscription well known from Poussin, *Et in Arcadia ego*, a reminder that, even in the idyllic world of pastoral, death is present. However, Wright's composite world of mixed delights was shortly to be overtaken by a second wave of garden buildings, though further out in the park (Wright's work was near the house), when Anson brought in James 'Athenian' Stuart to pursue a programme of Greek revival architecture.

Another major commission was at Stoke Gifford (now Stoke Park), Avon, for Lord Botetort and Elizabeth, now the Dowager Duchess of Beaufort. Wright designed both house and garden, and by way of demonstrating his versatility and capacity to surprise he laid out a classical landscape on a considerable scale, described as '*Epic* space', and with an elegiac theme suggested by a tomb, an obelisk and a monument based on an original at Albano. It was therefore quite a literary garden, somewhat in the spirit of the Leasowes, Worcestershire. The planting was also planned with great care and attention. Altogether it is a far cry from Wright's usual small-scale rococo work, but some of the elements are unmistakably Wright — the exceptionally serpentine walks, the separate compartments — and the architecture was as idiosyncratic as ever. The Horatian monument had four obelisks; Bladud's Temple was a typical piece of grotesquery, having a rustic exterior with a mysterious inscription over the entrance and mathematical problems drawn out on the floor; and a cascade tunnel 30 feet (9 metres) long bears traces of a grotto-type decoration.

The garden of Halswell, Somerset (pronounced 'Haswell'), is an intriguing composite of classical, Gothic and rustic features. Planned by Sir Charles Kemeys Tynte over a period of 44 years (1740-84), the garden gave scope to a number of architects and designers including Robert Adam, Henry Keene and Thomas Prowse. The involvement of Wright is not yet proven, but Tynte subscribed to his book of *Arbours* and there are three, if not four, structures which carry Wright's stamp. The Druid's Temple, a thatched rustic hut, went up in 1756 but was destroyed in the 1950s. It bears a close resemblance to the engraving on the title page of *Arbours*, published the previous year. A rockwork screen or grotto at the far end of the lake formed a dam and incorporates a number of niches and a large central arch with rough rock voussoirs. There is a Bath-stone bridge in Mill Wood which also forms a dam, again with a central arch, this time with large rusticated bands. These

*The Bath House at Wrest Park, Bedfordshire, attributed to Thomas Wright.*

two, the screen and the bridge, correspond to two of Wright's drawings in the Avery collection. The Rotunda, known as 'Mrs Busby's Temple' (1755), could also possibly be by Wright, although the form was common enough and could have been by many a hand.

As a totality the miniature garden at Hampton Court House, Middlesex, is a perfect expression of rococo, but although Wright was responsible this garden will be treated on its own in the final chapter. The owner was Lord Halifax, who also owned Horton, Northamptonshire, where Wright built an extraordinary Menagerie which, despite its name, was multi-purpose. It contained a small zoo, walled off from the central chamber, and two small side pavilions. The banqueting chamber has particularly fine rococo plasterwork attributed to Thomas Roberts of Oxford and, significantly, includes the signs of the zodiac and a sunburst effect in the centre of the design, reminding us of Wright's interests in the heavens.

At Wrest Park, Bedfordshire, Wright drew up plans for a garden which was already well established. It was a formal garden dominated by the long axial canal and the pavilion by Thomas Archer (1709-11) at one end. 'Capability' Brown formed a sinuous lake snaking around the garden and put in some perimeter plantings, but the heart of the garden, with its intersecting *allées*, bowling green and so on was left intact. Shortly after Brown's involvement (1758-60) Wright was brought in, apparently to create more away-from-centre embellishments. The most intriguing, and the only one that survives, is the Bath House, to one side of the original house (though Walpole attributed it to Brown rather than Wright). This is a double building, one part of which is a circular thatched edifice of uneven stone, containing a room with a floor patterned with knuckle bones. This presumably was an anteroom or changing room for the bath itself, which adjoins this chamber. The bath is covered by an openwork dome of stone, giving jagged-frame views of the gardens.

Wright's concentration on rustic led to 'primitive' works being designed by others, such as the Bark Temple at Exton Park, Leicestershire, constructed of wood but covered with bark (it has proved impossible to date this exactly). Hermitages were often composed of simple primitive materials — logs, tree trunks and roots, thatch — to give the idea that the hermit himself had created his dwelling out of whatever lay close to hand. A good example was the Hermitage at Painshill, Surrey, where a hermit engaged by Charles Hamilton stayed for three weeks before escaping to a local inn at Cobham. And the Hermitage at Hagley, Worcestershire, made of tree roots, had a seat described by Dr Pococke in 1751 as 'adorned with bones and embellished with a motto made of snail shells'.

*Garden at Woodside, Berkshire, with Orangery. Watercolour by Thomas Robins, c.1750. (Private collection. Photograph: Sotheby's.)*

*Pan's Lodge, near Painswick, Gloucestershire. Watercolour by Thomas Robins, 1758. (Courtesy of Lord Dickinson.)*

# Gothic

The Gothic revival in the eighteenth century, sometimes spelled 'Gothick' to distinguish it from the late Georgian and Victorian movement of the same name, which was a more serious matter affecting the architecture of houses and large buildings, has a variety of motivations behind it. One undoubtedly strong factor was political, the search for a style which embodied older native virtues that appeared to be lost under the current Whig government of Sir Robert Walpole. Another was pride in a tradition that was indigenous and had produced lasting masterpieces, both secular and ecclesiastical. There was also a sense of continuity and of evoking the spirit of the middle ages, perhaps in an escapist way. It also provided a foil and contrast, especially in gardens, to the Roman classicism and Italianate Palladianism that tended to predominate early on.

Horace Walpole's house at Strawberry Hill, Middlesex (from 1748), is often taken as a starting point of Gothic revival, yet this had its birth in gardens more than twenty years before. Alfred's Hall, in Cirencester Park, Gloucestershire, was devised by Alexander Pope and Lord Bathurst from 1721, and this was a reconstruction of a medieval house using some genuine materials — windows from the demolished Sapperton church, for example. It was effective enough to deceive antiquarians and was on occasion known as Arthur's Hall, giving it an even longer spurious lineage. The Gothic façade at Shotover, Oxfordshire, dates from the 1720s too, although there is some dispute as to whether it is an example of Oxford 'collegiate Gothic', spilling over from the colleges themselves, rather than Gothic revival. The mason at Shotover, William Townesend, had helped in college restoration.

William Kent used Gothic in some of his buildings, both as an essay in a different form and, where appropriate, for the historical 'feel' of the style in a particular place. Thus, at Esher Place, Surrey, he added Gothic wings and Gothic decoration to the existing real medieval Gothic of Waynflete's Tower. His Merlin's Cave at Richmond, Surrey, was thatched Gothic, and this building, containing wax figures of Queen Elizabeth I, Merlin and others, has been interpreted as a political statement, once again reinforcing the old values as exemplified by Gothic at the expense of the modern.

Kent's serpentine rill at Rousham, Oxfordshire, has already been mentioned. This, combined with his use of Gothic and other styles (he had a penchant for Egyptian as well), marks him out, if not as a rococo designer himself, at least as a forerunner of rococo. He showed the possibilities of experimenting with form and shape, although his prime allegiance, after ten years in Italy, was to Italian classicism. His interior decoration, often rich and exuberant, is pre-rococo in its symmetry but points towards the floridity of rococo, as do some of his designs for silverware. His splendid ornate barge built for Frederick, Prince of Wales, is perhaps baroque rather than rococo.

Many designers of garden buildings from the 1730s or 1740s onwards cultivated Gothic forms, generally characterised by the pointed arch. It has been argued that Gothic — the predominant form for follies — was the English equivalent to rococo, which implies that rococo was a form basically alien to the English, but it is possible to see rococo and Gothic as sometimes synonymous.

The type of Gothic which stretches across to overlap with rococo is most often that which uses the ogee curve. While simple Gothic can sometimes assume a rococo hue by virtue of other factors, for example size (see the Gothic seat at Painswick, Gloucestershire, final chapter), it is the ogee curve, with its suggestion of the oriental and its upsweeping concave form, that most readily lends itself to fanciful architecture. It was not a new invention, however, and a much flatter form of the curve is found in Tudor architecture. There is an ogee gable on the Red House at Painswick, and Sanderson Miller made good use of the motif at Enville, Staffordshire, and elsewhere. Henry Keene, working after Batty Langley, designed a striking ogee screen in Hartlebury Chapel, Worcestershire.

*Gothic Temple, Painshill, Surrey. (Photograph by Bill Owen: courtesy of the Painshill Park Trust.)*

A particularly memorable use of ogee form in a garden building is to be found in the Gothic Temple at Painshill, Surrey, *c*.1760. The architect is unknown, but candidates include Henry Keene, who designed the Turkish Tent there; Robert Adam, who drew designs for the ceiling and a pedestal for the Temple of Bacchus also at Painshill, and who used Gothic in some of his Scottish work; and Charles Hamilton himself, the owner and designer of the gardens. This building, with its lightness of colour, wood made to look like stone, slight buttresses, ogee arches, some of which have screens and others not, quatrefoil windows and painted fan vaulting is the essence of garden rococo.

Another example is the so-called White Tower at Hawkstone, Shropshire (*c*.1770). It is a castellate brick building which has long since lost any trace of whiteness, but the ogee form is used tellingly in interior arches. Frescoes of the four seasons once adorned the inside walls. Robin Hood's Hut at Halswell, Somerset (1765), also demonstrates lively use of the ogee both in the arches of the portico and in the windows on each side. This building is presumed to have been designed by Henry Keene for Sir Charles Kemeys Tynte — a preliminary design for it by Keene exists in the Victoria and Albert Museum.

The Needle's Eye at Wentworth Woodhouse, South Yorkshire, *c*.1780, is half pyramid, half obelisk. It is said to have been the result of a wager that a coach could not pass through the eye of a needle — a good rococo reason for building it. The 'eye' is, fittingly, in the form of an ogee arch.

A late piece of ogee Gothic, *c*.1800, is the Umbrello at Great Saxham Hall, Suffolk, which is highly unusual in being constructed of Coade stone. Some other late eighteenth-century work exists in the Bristol area, at Arnos Castle, Ashton Court and in the Gazebo at Ham Green Hospital, a small construction of local rubble stone with ogee lintels. But the most extraordinary folly of all is in Scotland — the Pineapple at Dunmore, Central Region, where the entire dome is a giant version of that fruit. The windows below are in ogee form.

'Toy Gothic' is in evidence at Fort Henry, Exton Park, Leicestershire. This is a mock fort, where boats would engage in representations of naval battles. This practice was by no means uncommon, and at West Wycombe, Buckinghamshire, Sir Francis Dashwood would similarly amuse himself on the lake, where he kept a fleet of four vessels, a battery of guns and a fort. Jolivet's 1752 survey of the grounds shows in addition Don Quixote's Castle, an island citadel in another lake below the cascade, resembling the forts of the military architect Vauban.

*(Facing page) Interior of Gothic Temple, Painshill, Surrey, showing fan vaulting. (Courtesy of the Painshill Park Trust.)*

*(Left)  Gothic arch on grotto hill, Hawkstone, Shropshire.*
*(Right)  Temple of the Winds, West Wycombe, Buckinghamshire.*

The Castle of rubble construction that gave Castle Hill, Devon, its name (*c*.1735-40) is also a sham fort, originally with a walled keep. Functional farm buildings — deer pens, kennels, barns, cowsheds — would often have a Gothic façade. Fort Putnam, Greystoke, Cumbria, is a farm and a toy fort at the same time, named after one of the sites of the American War of Independence.

A collection of mid-century oddities, mixing styles but based on Gothic, is to be found, in a derelict state, at Hackfall, North Yorkshire. This was a 'picturesque' garden, swooping down the inside of a great bowl to the river Ure at the foot, giving dramatic views and containing spectacular effects such as a 40 foot (12 metre) waterfall within it. Mowbray Castle at Hackfall is a Gothic octagon but with irregular, jagged masonry; Mowbray Point appears to be a classically pedimented building from the fields above the bowl but had Gothic decoration within, including ogee-arched alcoves, and as a further surprise appeared to have three massive Roman arches when viewed from below on the other side; and Fisher's Hall was a tufa-covered building with a Gothic door.

At West Wycombe there were strange buildings of several kinds, including a dovecote that was shaped to look like a circular temple from one side. A Gothic creation was St Crispin's Cottage, a shoemaker's dwelling disguised as a Gothic church, complete with spire.

The vogue for Gothic was assisted considerably by the promulgation of pattern books. These were books of designs for buildings and other artefacts which an owner could copy or modify for his own use. The idea was not new: Italian Renaissance architects such as Serlio and Palladio had produced architectural volumes which would include plans and elevations of existing buildings together with suggested designs. But the pattern book flourished in the eighteenth century, particularly in relation to garden buildings which could be put up relatively quickly and cheaply.

Pattern books embraced all styles. Batty Langley's *Gothic Architecture Improved...* (1747) was followed by Thomas Wright in the 1750s with the two folios already mentioned and by a host of minor figures eager to exploit the craze. The brothers William and John Halfpenny wrote a number of books, and several others added their own contribution. The best known of the books are listed here:

Chambers, William. *Designs of Chinese Buildings, &c.* 1757.
Decker, Paul. *Chinese Architecture Civil and Ornamental.* 1759.
— *Gothic Architecture.* 1759.
Edwards, George, and Darly, Matthew. *A New Book of Chinese Designs.* 1754.
Halfpenny, William and John. *Rural Architecture in the Chinese Taste.* 1750, 1752, 1755.
— *New Designs for Chinese Temples etc.* 1750-2.
— *Chinese and Gothic Architecture Properly Ornamented.* 1752.
— *Rural Designs in the Gothick Taste.* 1752.
Langley, Batty (and Thomas). *Gothic Architecture Improved....* 1747.
— *The Country Gentleman's Pocket Companion.* 1753.
Lightoler, Thomas. *The Gentleman and Farmer's Architect.* 1762.
Over, Charles. *Ornamental Architecture in the Gothic, Chinese and Modern Taste.* 1758.
Overton, T. C. *Original Designs for Temples.* 1746.
Wright, Thomas. *Universal Architecture.* 1755, 1758.
Wrighte, William. *Grotesque Architecture....* 1767.

From this it will be seen that the bewildered landowner had an array of styles from which to choose. There is no doubt that pattern books were used: some examples have already been noticed (for example the Druid's Temple at Halswell), and the Gothic Temple at Bramham, West Yorkshire (1750), came from one of Langley's designs.

It may seem that such a hotchpotch of styles would create absence of style, but eclecticism, and even the juxtaposition of different forms, can itself be one sign of rococo. A mixture can upset expectation and give the air of a capricious plan.

Just as Francis Coventry had satirised the rococo garden (or its owners) generally, so gardens filled with pattern-book designs were liable
to ridicule. Robert Lloyd's *The Cit's Country Box* (1757) disparages
chinoiserie, Gothic and Halfpenny's pattern bridges:

> 'The trav'ler with amazement sees
> A temple, Gothic or Chinese,
> With many a bell, and tawdry rag on
> And crested with a sprawling dragon;
> A wooden arch is bent astride
> A ditch of water, four feet wide,
> With angles, curves and zig-zag lines
> From Halfpenny's exact designs.'

Classical or Palladian designs have not been allocated a separate
chapter, since they do not fit readily into a rococo scheme, but they
cannot be excluded from consideration. Robert Adam, whose work
would not normally be described as rococo, came close to it in some of
his garden buildings, mainly those in multi-purpose usage. The Tea-
house Bridge at Audley End, Essex (1782-3), is a sort of Palladian
bridge with a superstructure yet it is a bridge from one side only. It is
also a loggia or small room for the taking of tea. Equally unusual is
Adam's Fishing Pavilion at Kedleston, Derbyshire (1771). The main
chamber is intended both for fishing from and for dining in, while lower
wings serve for mooring boats. A chamber beneath contains a stone
bath filled from an underground spring. The pavilion as a whole is
characteristic of Adam's neo-classical elegance, but the feeling is rococo.
Adam's tall, slim Brizlee Tower at Alnwick, Northumberland, could
be claimed to be rococo in some respects. Its rich exterior decoration is
medieval but culled from many sources. It contains niches, carvings,
arcades and windows in an elaborate several-storeyed structure that had
at least an origin which is truly rococo in spirit. It is said to have been
modelled on a cake made for the first Duke of Northumberland, who
was so delighted that he wanted an exact replica as a permanent land-
mark in the park. And at Culzean, Strathclyde, there is an assortment of
follies, mostly by Adam, which can be seen in its totality as a rococo
collection.
The Temple of Diana at Weston Park, Staffordshire, was designed by
James Paine. It is an orangery on one side, with an Adam ceiling, and a
temple on the other, with a bathroom, living quarters upstairs and a
central chamber where the chocolate-box rococo manner of the paintings
of Diana by Columba is complemented by asymmetrical loops and
garlands in the ceiling decoration.

# Chinoiserie

The phenomenon of chinoiserie in gardens coincides with the rococo period, although examples occur both earlier and later. In its spirit of fantasy and its upward-turning curves it clearly has a direct relation to rococo even though it stands as a genre in its own right. Not all Chinese buildings fit into rococo, and the best known of all, the Pagoda at Kew, Surrey, might be considered to come within the category only for some of its decoration, for as a building it is too large and dominant. When we think of rococo chinoiserie, it is much more on the scale of the small temple in Robins's watercolour of Woodside, Old Windsor, Berkshire (see cover).

The whole question of the influence of China on the English landscape garden is a complex one and is still the subject of debate. Certainly there had been a taste for things Chinese in Britain for well over a century, as decorative objects, ceramics, lacquered cabinets and so on came from the east and created a vogue for such designs. Some of the scenes depicted on these objects would be from gardens, and missionaries or members of embassies, such as Nieuhof, drew Chinese gardens, prints of which would find a ready circulation. It has been suggested that some of the Chinese rock formations, particularly those which were piled up deliberately, might have influenced certain similar formations in England (for example the rockwork cascade at West Wycombe, Buckinghamshire). Sir William Temple's anglicised spelling from the Chinese, *sharawadgi* (contained in his book *Upon the Gardens of Epicurus*, 1685), introduced another possibly influential dimension — the idea of variety, novelty and surprise.

Leaving aside the influence or otherwise of actual Chinese gardens, there was a great deal of chinoiserie to be seen, though how authentically Chinese is quite another matter. Richard Bateman, who has already been mentioned as a pioneer of flower gardens, was also the instigator of chinoiserie — Horace Walpole said that he 'was the founder of the Sharawadgi taste in England'. From as early as the 1730s, and certainly by 1740, Bateman had a number of Chinese features in his garden at Old Windsor. Dr Richard Pococke, on his travels through England, visited Old Windsor in 1754 and left a helpful description. He mentions a piece of grotesque shellwork, a Chinese alcove seat, a Chinese covered bridge and, further on, a greenhouse in the Chinese taste. These features enlivened the flower gardens, parterre, groves and meadows which surrounded the house. Bateman's Chinese pavilion mingled styles to an astonishing degree. There were Dutch tiles, rococo plasterwork, flint facings, a hint of Indian in the roof, classical porticoes and a Chinese lantern tower.

*Chinese bridge, Painshill, Surrey. (Photograph by Bill Owen: courtesy of the Painshill Park Trust.)*

Unfortunately the Chinese elements disappeared in Bateman's own time. Fired with enthusiasm for Gothic, and fresh from his creation of Strawberry Hill, Walpole browbeat Bateman into replacing chinoiserie with Gothic: 'I preached so effectually that his every pagoda took the veil.'

Another early Chinese feature was the Chinese pavilion at Stowe, Buckinghamshire, dating from 1738. This has twice been moved, first to Wotton, Buckinghamshire, and then to Harristown in Ireland. The murals were by the Venetian Sleter, whose work at Stowe also included lurid interiors in the Temple of Venus. A few years later a pagoda was erected by Benjamin Hyett at Marybone, Gloucester.

From the 1740s onwards the trickle of chinoiserie became a torrent. At Shugborough, Staffordshire, Thomas Anson erected a Chinese house which was modelled on drawings made during his brother's sea voyages to the Far East. Examples elsewhere were westernised ideas of China, which the popularity of the pattern books had helped to make widespread. At Studley Royal, North Yorkshire, a discrete area was set aside for Chinese effects, including rockwork and a pavilion, while at Virginia Water, Surrey, the Chinese bridge and pavilion on Chinese

Island were complemented by the *Mandarin*, a yacht with Chinese superstructure.

Apart from Woodside, Robins depicted other ephemeral Chinese pavilions such as that at Honington, Warwickshire. Some were very flimsy indeed and could be taken down and re-erected, such as the Chinese Tent now at Boughton, Northamptonshire, where the materials, painted oilcloth and wood, have had to be renewed from time to time.

By the 1750s the fashion had become so widespread that Walpole exclaimed that at Wroxton, Oxfordshire, there were 'several paltry Chinese buildings and bridges, which have the merit or demerit of being the progenitors of a very numerous race all over the kingdom', though his view was coloured by his own preference for Gothic. Despite his feeling that there was already too much chinoiserie about, the greatest purveyor of the style was yet to come. Sir William Chambers had been to Canton as a teenage cabin boy and claimed to have seen Chinese gardens while on shore. His two books *Designs of Chinese Buildings...* (1757) and *A Dissertation on Oriental Gardening* (1772) were immensely successful and popular, even more so in France than in Britain. However, apart from the overt purpose of disseminating Chinese designs, the second book is a clothing for an attack on 'Capability' Brown and what was seen as his insipidity of style. William Mason's *An Heroic Epistle to Sir William Chambers* (1773) defended Brown by burlesquing Chambers's notions:

'No! let Barbaric glories feast his eyes
August Pagodas round his palace rise .........
Monkies shall climb our trees, and lizards crawl;
Huge dogs of Tibet bark in yonder grove,
Here parrots prate, there cats make cruel love.'

This echoes Robert Lloyd's dismissal of bells and dragons in *The Cit's Country Box*, quoted in the previous chapter.

Chambers put into practice his ideas of Chinese designs in some of the buildings he drew up for Princess Augusta at Kew. The buildings fell into two groups, the classical and the oriental. Of the former several remain, but the Pagoda is the sole survivor of the exotica, although the Japanese Gateway nearby, dating from 1912, recreates at least some of the flavour of an 'eastern' area. One of the original buildings, the House of Confucius, may date from an earlier period and be by Goupy, but Chambers was responsible for the Pagoda, the Alhambra, the Mosque and the open T'ing Pavilion, which were grouped as an oriental collection. The Japanese Gateway was placed on the site of the Mosque, on a small knoll.

At Amesbury Abbey, Wiltshire, there is a Chinese summerhouse over a bridge, designed by Chambers in 1772 for the Duchess of Queensbury, possibly on the site of an earlier Chinese pavilion.

Just as Thomas Robins portrayed gardens through rococo frames, there was an artist who tried to give gardens a flavour of chinoiserie by means of the way he depicted them. The painter Pillement, whose sketches and paintings are full of Chinese birds, figures and so on, executed two views of Oatlands, Surrey, which were engraved by William Elliot. He peoples this most English of landscape scenes, across the flat Thames valley, with women in Chinese costume with parasols; the men, however, retain their normal Georgian dress.

Bridges of the period, commonly with criss-cross latticework, are sometimes described as Chinese, though the same designs are often labelled rustic or native. The Chinese bridge at Painshill, Surrey, has been described as 'Chinese Chippendale', for instance. Garden furniture could be Chinese as well, and there are some extreme examples in the pattern books.

Chinoiserie did not die with the passing of rococo. Late in the century there was a striking assemblage at Woburn Abbey, Bedfordshire, including the Chinese Dairy by Henry Holland, followed in 1837 by a pagoda (much shorter than its cousin at Kew). About the same time Alton Towers, Staffordshire, had a fine cast iron pagoda erected.

Chinoiserie decoration sometimes included monkeys, though *singerie* almost constitutes a genre in its own right and does not have to have anything to do with China. Congreve's monument at Stowe is in the form of a monkey looking in a mirror, and the simian imitation of human behaviour is often exploited in amusing or playful ways. The supreme example is on Monkey Island in the Thames at Bray, Berkshire, where the Rustic Lodge contains a room with murals by Clermont which depict scenes in which monkeys take the place of people indulging in various country pursuits — shooting, punting boats and so on.

In addition to Chinese, there were other exotic styles which similarly could evoke fanciful and mysterious associations of the Orient. There was a Turkish Tent of canvas at Painshill, an inferior copy at Stourhead, Wiltshire, and a more substantial one in Vauxhall Gardens, London. A Turkish Tent surmounted by a crescent moon stands at Wotton but in poor condition. In Chambers's collection of eastern buildings at Kew, we have seen that there were both a Mosque and an Alhambra, each of which owed as much stylistically to rococo as to its supposed origin.

Indian as a style did not catch on to any extent. The Royal Pavilion at Brighton, East Sussex, was inspired by the Indian themes at Sezincote, Gloucestershire, where the architecture of the house is carried through several of the garden works — a conservatory, the bridge, decorated

*Chinese House, Shugborough, Staffordshire.*
*Chinese Dairy, Woburn Abbey, Bedfordshire.*

with Brahminee bulls, an Indian temple containing a figure of the goddess Souriya and a bronze serpent coiled round a column.

Vauxhall Gardens was not the only one of the London pleasure gardens to contain manifestations of rococo. A small part of Vauxhall, with a few of its 'supper boxes', was recreated as the centrepiece of the exhibition on English Rococo at the Victoria and Albert Museum. The garden itself, strictly geometrical in the layout of its walks, could not be described as rococo, but some of the elements it contained certainly were. The statues of Milton and Handel were by Louis François Roubiliac, already noted as a sculptor with a rococo approach, and the supper-box paintings were mostly by Francis Hayman, who, far from providing anodyne decoration, portrayed scenes with a surprising undercurrent of risk or tension, such as games on the ice. Apart from the Turkish Tent, there was a Temple of Comus (to pick up the Miltonic theme); the Rotunda had rococo decoration within; and one of the semicircles of supper boxes was in a bizarre stylistic mixture that can be summed up as Chinese Gothic.

Another of the London pleasure gardens, Ranelagh, had a small stretch of water surrounding a pavilion which again was something of a hybrid. Called the Chinese House in prints, it had a number of masks of Italian nature and has been described as Venetian. There were thus several constructions which created surprise and broke the rules, and this was one characteristic aspect of rococo.

# Sanderson Miller

That gifted and inventive amateur architect Sanderson Miller (1716-80), whose work covers the years of the mid eighteenth century, typifies much of the rococo spirit. Adventurous and sometimes extravagant in style, he accomplished a great number of commissions, many of which remain as his memorials. He is remembered principally for his creation of castles (mostly built as ruins) but his range of style was considerably wider, though often tinged with an atmosphere of romance and excitement. Like a number of his contemporaries, he was self-taught as an architect, and his commissions were mainly for his friends. His work was concentrated in the Midlands but later extended out to Surrey, Norfolk and Gloucestershire. Politically he stood with the Whig opposition, among whom were several influential friends who were also involved in the new landscape garden movement. He had a gift for friendship, and his own Octagonal Tower at Radway, near Edgehill, Warwickshire, the first of the 'castles' to be built, was the venue for entertaining his many friends. No doubt the sight of this building, combined with Miller's hospitality, inspired some of those friends to ask him to create a similar work for them. His commissions came mostly in the period 1748-60, though in the 1750s he was afflicted with severe bouts of melancholy that caused him such acute distress that in 1759 he had to be placed briefly in a private asylum. However, he made a good recovery.

In several cases Miller designed the house, though only Hagley Hall, Worcestershire, now survives. In other instances, such as Lacock Abbey, Wiltshire, Miller altered part of the building or would undertake some small task such as refurbishing a monument in a church. But the garden was where his genius could flourish at its most unfettered.

The list of his garden works, definite and probable, is impressive. He is likely to have been responsible for several buildings in the major landscapes of Enville (Staffordshire), Wroxton, near Banbury (Oxfordshire), Farnborough Hall (Warwickshire), Hagley (Worcestershire), Honington Hall, (Warwickshire), Packington Hall (Warwickshire) and his own Radway Grange (Warwickshire). In addition there were several memorable single or isolated works in a number of gardens such as his ruined castles at Wimpole, Cambridgeshire, and on Claverton Down, near Bath, Avon, a classical building at Croome Court, Worcestershire, where he worked with 'Capability' Brown, and a Gothic gateway at the entrance to the grounds of Lacock Abbey, where he remodelled the great hall in the Gothic style.

At Hagley Miller designed the house for George, Lord Lyttelton, which was built in 1756-7, a Palladian-style mansion based on Colen

*Ruined castle, Hagley, Worcestershire.*

Campbell's Houghton Hall in Norfolk. The surprise is that this slightly severe and 'correct' house contains a riot of rococo plasterwork decoration within. In the park, on the eminence of one of the encircling hills, stands the castle which was completed from Miller's design in 1748. This was a development of the idea of a medieval fortress which Miller had first embodied at his own home at Radway Grange. As with Alfred's Hall in Cirencester Park, Gloucestershire, there were some genuine old components — some medieval stonework from Halesowen Abbey, West Midlands, was incorporated at Hagley. What counted was that it was a ruined castle, serving both as an eyecatcher from a distance and to give a distinct dynastic feeling of antiquity to the Lyttelton estate, a suggestion that it was a relic from the family's past history. Horace Walpole said of it that it 'had the true rust of the barons' wars', thereby praising it as pastiche but indicating that the eighteenth century took its illusions and associations seriously. There is a certain ambivalence, akin to the suspension of disbelief in a theatre, in acknowledging that such a building was false yet accepting its impression of authenticity.

The castle is a substantial piece of work, which might be deemed to deny its admittance as rococo. But in its artificiality, its theatricality and its pretence, and in the consequent response it evokes, it belongs at least to the same world of fantasy.

At Wimpole too there is a ruined castle, which has an interesting history. Miller designed it for Lord Hardwicke in 1752, but it was not put up until *c.*1770, based on Miller's designs. Miller was still alive but no longer architecturally active. The date of execution coincides with 'Capability' Brown's work on the grounds, when, in terms of fashion, the castle was slightly out of date. It is possible that Brown remembered his former colleague from Croome Court days, but more likely that the second Earl Hardwicke was concerned to fulfil his father's vision of the park on that side of the house as a pictorial scene in which the castle would dominate from a height in the distance in a direct line from the house. Brown's lake with Chinese bridge delineated the line of the middle ground across from left to right.

Miller's spiritual ancestor was Sir John Vanbrugh, who foreshadowed so many aspects of the landscape garden long before they became established. Vanbrugh brought his theatrical side to bear in his architecture and built massive sham fortifications at Castle Howard, North Yorkshire — castellated walls with turrets and bastions. Nor did Miller invent the sham castle, for apart from Vanbrugh's castellate belvedere

*(Left) Game larder at Farnborough Hall, Warwickshire.*

*(Right) Dovecote at Wroxton, Oxfordshire, modelled on Guy's Tower at Warwick Castle.*

*Gothic summerhouse, Enville, Staffordshire, before restoration. (Courtesy of the Royal Commission on the Historical Monuments of England.)*

*Interior of boathouse, Enville, Staffordshire (now destroyed). (Courtesy of the Royal Commission on the Historical Monuments of England.)*

at Claremont, Surrey (*c*.1715), Stainborough Castle at Wentworth, South Yorkshire (1728-30), has a keep, a bailey and a curtain wall with towers at intervals.

Enville was one of three great gardens that visitors to the western Midlands had to see. The others were Hagley and the Leasowes, Worcestershire. In the ownership of the Earl of Stamford, Enville Hall was surrounded by a landscaped park of varied terrain which allowed for spectacular cascades and breathtaking views. Hard evidence is lacking for Miller's definite contribution to the various buildings, but he is likely to have had a hand in much of the work, which included a Gothic summerhouse (restored), a hermitage (almost totally collapsed), a classical pavilion with square rusticated columns, a Gothic gateway (restored), a Gothic boathouse over a bridge (destroyed by a tree in the 1970s) and Shenstone's Chapel, named after the owner of the Leasowes, who was a frequent visitor to Enville. Two buildings in particular exhibit rococo in a number of features, both externally and in the decoration inside. These are the Gothic summerhouse and the boathouse, both of which demonstrate the fanciful end of the Gothic scale. The summerhouse, variously referred to also as the Billiard Room or Museum, has ogee arches and rose windows somewhat in the manner of Batty Langley, with intricate interior decoration. The boathouse, a small octagonal building, was a capriccio, the interior pure rococo.

The gardens of Wroxton (for Lord North) preserve a good deal of Miller's work. The area in which rococo was concentrated includes the grand cascade, restored in the early 1980s, with a smaller cascade below it, a serpentine stream and the foundations of a Chinese bridge, one of several Chinese features that were originally present, as shown in an engraving of 1751 (two bridges and three buildings: a lodge, a Chinese house and a small open Chinese seat with a tent roof). It would be good to know if Miller designed all these, for he experimented with chinoiserie at Honington, and they would fit into his rococo thinking. Elsewhere there is a (restored) ruined arch, set at a distance as an eyecatcher, and an obelisk; a Gothic temple on a mount has long since disappeared. Most important however, is the Gothic dovecote, which is a miniature version of Guy's Tower at Warwick Castle, the model also for Miller's own tower at Radway. The small copy at Wroxton is therefore very much a Miller signature, a toy copy of an imitation.

One of the happiest surviving displays of Miller's varied art is the collection of buildings dating from the 1750s along and near the long terrace walk at Farnborough Hall, north of Banbury. An Ionic temple nestles against the hill just below the rim of the terrace, while a strange little hexagonal game larder stands slightly away from the terrace. An obelisk terminates the terrace itself.

But the jewel of the collection is the Oval Pavilion, a most unusual, if not unique, shape with a tiny upper room which contains a profusion of rococo plasterwork by William Perritt, white on a blue background. Perritt had undertaken similar decoration in the house, so this is a pleasing example of a garden pavilion carrying on a theme or motif from the house into the grounds.

As we have seen from the chapter on Thomas Robins, who depicted Miller's landscape at Honington, the latter was a garden which rivalled Wroxton for rococo display. Chinoiserie, rockwork, cascades, small buildings, all within a limited space, bring Honington close, stylistically, to Wroxton and demonstrate the characteristics of Miller's rococo patterns.

Miller may have been the most famous exponent of ruins but he did not have a monopoly. Purpose-built ruins made their appearance in many gardens for varying effects. A ruin of a classical building would both evoke the spirit of ancient Rome and testify to the passing of time and the decay of all things. Charles Hamilton's ruined Mausoleum at Painshill, Surrey, was intended to have this effect. It was built as a derelict Roman triumphal arch and housed some genuine antique pieces of sculpture, while Roman altars and sarcophagi were placed on the lawn nearby. The most commonly found ruins, however, were ecclesiastical, purporting to be medieval. Thus at Painshill there is also a ruined abbey, while at Mount Edgcumbe, Cornwall, a ruined chapel overlooks the sea. William Shenstone had a ruined priory at the Leasowes, and Philip Southcote a ruined chapel at Woburn Farm, Surrey, where there may have been some idea of paying tribute to the pre-Reformation religious past, Southcote being a Catholic. A sham chapel was erected at Crowcombe, Somerset, from the stone of a demolished chapel. No doubt part of the inspiration for putting ruined church buildings in a garden landscape came from the real Cistercian ruins in North Yorkshire, especially Rievaulx Abbey, the views of which were carefully controlled from the terrace walk on the cliff above, and Fountains Abbey, long planned to be the climax of the view at Studley Royal.

Now it cannot be claimed that ruins have any architectural connection with rococo, but their effect could be consonant with a rococo scene. They would certainly demonstrate surprise, irregularity and illusion in appearing to be something that they were not and would thus contribute to the overall imaginative landscapes of the rococo period. The most extraordinary was perhaps the Ruin at Fawley Court, Buckinghamshire, where a Gothic structure with ruined flint wall turns inside into a classical chamber with a rustic flavour and a flooring of sheep's knuckle bones.

# From formal to rococo: Belcombe Court and Carshalton House

It is the case that rococo gardens were not necessarily created either in a single period or *de novo*: some were converted to rococo in the mid eighteenth century, modifying an originally formal design. Two good examples of this are Belcombe Court, Bradford-on-Avon, Wiltshire, and Carshalton House, Surrey.

Belcombe Court was the home of the Yerbury family, clothmakers who had prospered in the wool industry that was so prominent in that region. It is a hilly spot, and the garden was laid out against the side of a slope. What we would now describe as the rococo garden is a tiny area adjacent to the back of the house, so that one can see from the windows all the elements at once, namely the rotunda, the crescent pool, the grotto and the Gothic cottage in the background. A further garden building, a rectangular temple, is at the top of the hill, out of sight of the rococo configuration.

We do not know for certain the sequence of events which led to the completion of this composition, since some crucial dating of the buildings is missing, but the likely evolution is as follows. The rotunda and pool were clearly built at the same time, which is known to have been during the 1730s. The Gothic cottage and grotto came later, possibly *c*.1770, from stylistic evidence, namely that the grotto resembles the work of Josiah Lane of Tisbury (the younger Lane), who, it will be remembered, created a number of grottoes, particularly in his home county of Wiltshire. There is no evidence that Lane himself designed it, but the rough, 'natural' appearance of the rock and the way it is built up are in the manner of the second half of the eighteenth century, not earlier.

Further evidence is that John Wood of Bath, when he described Belcombe, gave a date of slightly after 1734 to the rotunda, which he spoke of disparagingly, possibly because he had not been invited to design it (he had added a wing to the house). In his description of the garden there is no mention of the grotto, which he could not have missed if it had been built since it stands close to the rotunda, and which, had it been in existence, would have demanded attention and comment.

The supposition must be, therefore, that the rotunda and pool were built as part of a formal small-scale layout in the 1730s which was subsequently transformed into a rococo scene by the addition of the naturalistic grotto and the Gothic cottage behind. The final picture is indisputably rococo: small, asymmetrical, 'curious', whimsical. What

*Hermitage, Carshalton House, Surrey (postcard, c.1920). (Courtesy of the London Borough of Sutton.)*

*Lake, sham bridge and water tower at Carshalton House, Surrey. Engraving by William Watts, 1783. (Courtesy of the London Borough of Sutton.)*

is more, the earlier formal elements of pool and *tempietto* take on a rococo colouring by virtue of their juxtaposition with the later works.

The rotunda is similar to many elsewhere, although the pairs of columns close together mark it out as unusual (but certainly not unique). The placing by a pool is reminiscent of Edward Haytley's paintings of Beachborough House, Kent. The pool is presumably intended to be a crescent, though its recent adaptation as a swimming pool and subsequent restoration to the original form have resulted in a few straight edges. The pool changes from the formal crescent to a more natural pond in front of the grotto.

The Gothic cottage has a tiled roof although it was originally stone. This, like the grotto, is a feature more likely to have come from the later eighteenth century than the earlier, in tune with the developing taste for the rustic picturesque. It may have existed in an earlier form and then been Gothicised. The Gothic cottage at Stourhead, Wiltshire, for comparison, dates from well towards the end of the century, while the Nash/Repton concept of the 'village picturesque' did not get under way until the 1790s.

The grotto is on a smaller scale than its well known contemporaries previously discussed. It does, however, have two storeys, the upper deck being a kind of balcony, known as the Banqueting Room, although it is small and open. Jagged pieces of rock and stone serve as balustrade to this upper level. There is some dressing of tufa or spongestone. Below is a cave with side passages to it: the floor of the cave is studded with ammonites, and the water from the pool outside trickles between the paving slabs. The dampness would have confirmed Dr Samuel Johnson in his opinion that a grotto was an admirable

*Sham bridge, Carshalton House, Surrey. (Courtesy of the London Borough of Sutton.)*

*Rotunda and pool, Belcombe Court, Wiltshire.*

place — for toads. At Belcombe myriads of minute frogs swarm across the floor. Rock plants and other modern plantings of ferns and flowers make the grotto and its surroundings more attractive than it would have been originally, a stark craggy feature.

At Carshalton House Charles Bridgeman laid out a handsome garden, larger in area than at Belcombe, but certainly not on a landscape garden scale, for Sir John Fellowes, a director of the South Sea Company, *c.*1720. The garden was axial, concentrating on a straight canal from the house to an imposing water tower in the manner of Sir John Vanbrugh though possibly built by Henry Joynes. The only surviving plan of the grounds, by John Rocque somewhat later, is unclear and may possibly indicate a parallel canal. There were avenues of trees, statues and fountains.

Carshalton House had a number of owners during the century, including the much travelled Lord Anson, Thomas Walpole (cousin of Horace) and Theodore Broadhead, who held the property from 1782 to 1792. It is conjectured that the radical alterations that were made to the gardens occurred during the time of Walpole (1767-82). The finished appearance of the new style sitting on top of the old is given in William Watts's engraving of 1783. These alterations consisted of: (1) the obliteration of the canal; (2) its replacement by a 'natural' sinuous lake, roughly on a diagonal axis; (3) the termination of the lake at one end by

*Grotto, Belcombe Court, Wiltshire.*

a sham bridge; (4) the construction of a summerhouse beside the lake, later called 'The Hermitage'; (5) the realignment of the grotto/conduit entrance to face the diagonal lake.

Elements of rococo were brought in by these changes. The sham bridge is illusionist in giving the appearance that the water flows on, under and beyond it, by means of shadow which is created by burnt clinker or slag, the sort of industrial waste that was often used in grottoes. A rustic house stood for some time above the bridge. The lake is a waving line, but smaller than 'Capability' Brown's creations. The summerhouse/hermitage is a strange concoction which continues to baffle in terms of its purpose and usage. This most unusual building is now derelict. The wings are Victorian, while the original centre unit is of chalk on a brick core. It consists of a central chamber with a circular room off it — possibly an ice well, although there was a separate icehouse in the grounds — and a corridor curving round at the back. A date of 1749 is inscribed in the wall but is of dubious authenticity; a second date of 1769 is thought to be more feasible.

The water tower stands prominently in the new scene, as it did in the old. Although the style of architecture was by then out of fashion, the tower is not incongruous in its changed setting: it even has some interesting irregularity inasmuch as the back of the tower had to accommodate the wall along the street outside, which cuts across at an angle.

# The rococo garden: Painswick and Hampton Court House

The finest and fullest manifestations of the rococo garden are Painswick, near Stroud, Gloucestershire, and Hampton Court House, just inside Bushy Park, opposite Hampton Court Palace, Middlesex. Both contain much that is rococo, but they are very different and illustrate the range of what the term can cover.

Painswick is a garden in a hidden valley to one side of the house and with no obvious relationship to it. The present owner, Lord Dickinson, is an indirect descendant of the original owner in the eighteenth century, Benjamin Hyett, who had a comfortable inheritance and two properties in Painswick — Painswick House (known at the time as Buenos Aires from the sweet air that it is said to have enjoyed) and Pan's Lodge about a mile away, in addition to Marybone House, Gloucester. Hyett's father built the house but did not live long to savour the *buenos aires*. Benjamin inherited the house and a reasonable parcel of land (though modest by aristocratic standards). A painting of the garden at Painswick by Thomas Robins in 1748 shows the layout, which by 1980 had become obscured by undergrowth and deliberate planting over. A restoration plan, based on Robins's painting, was commenced in 1984, the intention being to bring the garden as far as possible back to Hyett's conception.

Robins's painting has to be approached with understanding. First, the angle of the garden is misleading, for the reality is a sloping, sinking valley. The plane has been tilted up in order to display it in pictorial form. Then, there is a puzzle concerning the exedra, the semicircular Gothic screen which appears top right in front of the trees. No foundations for this have been discovered, though one would have expected some sign of its existence, however slight. This suggests that the painting might have been of what was intended rather than executed or even that it represented the design itself, some of which was implemented and other parts not. This has given rise to a claim that Robins laid out the garden as well as depicting it. The arched façade to the left of the exedra has also disappeared, to be replaced by the classical seat there now, which was moved from elsewhere.

The area of the garden is about 6 acres (2.4 ha). It is thus not a particularly small garden, though most of the buildings have been scaled down in size from what they might be in a landscape park. The layout is formal, with a prominent straight central avenue forming the main axis. Other paths are also mostly straight, and there is a *patte d'oie* at the top of the valley (see the Robins plan, far right). However, the formal-

ity is countered by a lack of symmetry and balance between the
parts on each side of the axis, by
some serpentising of paths and
water, and above all by the buildings themselves. These constitute
a strange and idiosyncratic collection.

The Gothic Alcove is a small
wooden building terminating the
beech walk.  It is of triple-arch
form, the centre arch higher than
the others, all surmounted with
crenellations.  It is small in size
but fitted to the scale of the walk
leading up to it. It does not correspond exactly to what is depicted in
Robins's painting, which suggests
a change of form at the time or
afterwards.

The bath and adjacent spring
head form a nymphaeum, the
bathing pool of antiquity.  Originally the statue of Pan stood
beside it to reinforce the classical
allusion, and he is to be returned
there.

*Eagle House, Painswick, Gloucestershire.
Watercolour by Thomas Robins. (Courtesy
of Lord Dickinson.)*

The Doric seat has columns banded with rustication; what is less
common is the rustication within the pediment, paralleled perhaps only
by Richard Woods's use of tufa within the pediment of a folly at
Buckland House, Oxfordshire. The seat is the portico from the Pigeon
House.

The Eagle House unfortunately lost its superstructure of a pavilion
with Gothic windows, pinnacles and walls rendered in red. It is, however, due to be rebuilt during 1991.  The base is a recess set into the
terrace walk bank, but it is substantial enough to have niches, a chamber
and a castellated roof.

At some distance is the Pigeon House, not properly part of the 'secret
garden' but dating from the same time.  It is a two-storey octagonal
structure somewhat in the manner of William Kent.

Most rococo of all is the Red House at the eastern end.  This is sited at
the apex of a sort of *patte d'oie* — but instead of three or more straight
avenues converging at the point, one of the avenues is completely ser-

*Plan of Painswick gardens, Gloucestershire. Watercolour by Thomas Robins, 1748. (Courtesy of Lord Dickinson.)*

pentine, as Robins shows. The Red House itself is the oddest of all the buildings, a wilful piece of asymmetry which teases and perplexes. It is a 'hinged' building with two façades that face the two straight avenues. The façades are different: one has an ogee curve surmounted by a cross, together with recessed upright buttresses, and the other has a concave curve sweeping up to the pointed top, and only one window, contrasting with the two windows and door of the other. The label 'Red House' indicates that, like the Eagle House, it had a red finish. It is a unique work and stands at the topmost point of the garden as if to establish a tone of enigma from on high.

The Pan that used to stand by the plunge pool now greets the visitor just before entering the garden. The lead figure is supposed to be by John Van Nost and bears a family resemblance to the Pan at Rousham, Oxfordshire. It is particularly appropriate that Pan should be the resident deity, since he commands the revels at Pan's Lodge and also because Robins in the captions to his drawings calls Painswick

'Panswyke', the village of Pan. It is in accordance with the upsetting of expectation in the garden that Pan was not originally in a prominent position but slyly supervised events from the side.

The origin of the name of Painswick is somewhat unclear. A Pain Fitzjohn (died 1137) may have given his name to the village which was at that time called simply 'Wicke' or 'Wyke'. Another possible derivation is from the thirteenth-century appellation 'Wyke Pagani', which still lives on in the neighbouring Pagans Hill. So Robins's humorous suggestion of a connection with Pan may not be so far from the truth.

Robins's drawing of the garden is of special interest for its bordering too. In addition to the stems, tendrils, leaves and flowers (mostly native wild) with which we are familiar from other of his paintings, there is a motif of shells. These are closely related to rococo, as we have seen, with their convoluted curves and their use in early *rocaille* decoration. Such shell forms are referred to as *coquillage*. They therefore announce rococo even more strongly than usual in Robins's borders.

The view of Painswick from Pan's Lodge by Robins (1758) has once

*Painswick, Gloucestershire, from Pan's Lodge. Watercolour by Thomas Robins, 1758. (Courtesy of Lord Dickinson.)*

again a vividly rococo border, this time embellished by butterflies and peacock and pheasant feathers as well as leaves, stalks and flowers. The theme of this border is exotic — butterflies and plants from Mexico, Peru, the Canary Islands and so on. Pan is the 'Genius of the Place', leading the dance and the revelry. The view is of the whole village and church as well as the surrounding country.

From a garden of Pan we turn to a garden of Venus. The second Earl of Halifax, who happened conveniently to be Ranger of Bushy Park, obtained permission from himself to build a house just inside the boundary of the park, across what is now the A308 from Hampton Court Palace. The house, Hampton Court House, and its small grounds were established for Halifax's mistress, Mrs Donaldson, and it is to some extent a garden of love. The pool is roughly heart-shaped, and there is appropriate erotic symbolism in the grotto. A statue of Venus holds court in the grotto, which was restored from 1984 following extensive dereliction and damage, although there is no evidence for her original presence.

The garden is true rococo. It is much smaller than Painswick, and the designer was Thomas Wright, who knew better than anyone else how to create surprise and interest in such a limited space. As at Belcombe, the features of interest are all close to the house — the exedra, the grotto, the pool, the fountain arch, the 'icehouse'. A further structure, the openwork wrought iron Rose Temple, is Victorian but fits in well with the rococo spirit of the other features.

The house was built in 1757 and the garden was made a decade later. A short terrace walk from the house leads to a small tiered exedra of burnt clinker and stone of the sort that was also used for the exterior of the grotto and icehouse. The material thus gives the exedra a linking unity with the other features. It is now partly submerged in a rockery but was presumably originally a simple curved niche to terminate the walk. The use of burnt material, sometimes industrial waste, was, as we have seen, a common feature of rococo work of this period.

The pond has an irregular outline approximately in the shape of a heart. The grotto faces it on one side, and opposite is a fountain, which has now largely disappeared but remains in the form of the ruinous uprights of a rock arch.

The icehouse poses something of a mystery. A brick well is to be found in the base, but the presence of a room above with a fireplace — even if that was a later addition — suggests some alternative purpose. It is very much a colleague of the grotto — close by, and faced with the same burnt slag. It stands among trees on a raised mound.

Pride of place in the garden goes to the grotto, a superb, distinctive creation by Wright. The exterior of the title-page illustration in his book of grotto designs is similar to that of the grotto, and on the basis of the similarity the attribution to Wright was first made. The rusticity of the branchwork on the door has been taken from the illustration.

The grotto is built into a mound or bank, which is artificial. Ramps circle round at the back, rather as they did at Oatlands, Surrey. The two wings, which do not have the interior decoration of the grotto chamber itself, may possibly have been added later. The rockwork and rustication of the exterior comprise stone, burnt slag, pitted spongestone, chunks of rock and some adornment of shells and quartz. The basic core is of brick.

When the large door is opened, the surprise is total. A feast of colour and dramatic imagery greets the eye. The main chamber has an arched apsidal recess on each side and an alcove at the back, facing the door. Shells of all types, sizes and hues pour down the walls, while the ceiling of the chamber is a blue firmament with gilded stars and moon affixed. Both walls and ceiling have been reconstructed as far as possible from the evidence that existed before restoration: the colour of the original ceiling was known and some of the stars were still to be found, while the type of shells could be determined from the marks left behind in the lime mortar even though the shells themselves had almost entirely vanished. Where that was not possible, only shells known to have been available in the 1760s have been used. The floor is pebbled, as was often the case.

The Venus in the centre of the large scalloped shell in the alcove is new, although the shell itself would have suggested the presence of her spirit. The entire decoration conveys a sense of the cycles of time and growth, the ceiling being the sky and the apses representing dawn and evening, with light and dark coloured shells respectively. This apsidal decor is a modern conception but in keeping with what we know to have been there and with Wright's interests in astronomy.

About forty thousand shells were required, from as far afield as Africa and the West Indies as well as those native to Britain. The shapes and patterning of the shells suggest flowers and trees, which relate garden growth to the movement in the heavens that is portrayed by the rest of the grotto. The range of size and form of shell and coral is astonishing. Prominent use of large cowrie shells denotes their sexual significance.

In addition to shells, there is much mineral ornament, particularly on the columns. In the use of columns and recesses, the application of minerals and the shellwork generally, there is some resemblance to the grotto at Goldney, Avon. The decoration at Goldney was spread over a great many years, but it was well advanced by the time of Hampton Court House grotto and Wright may therefore have got some

*Grotto, Hampton Court House, Middlesex.*
*Interior of grotto, Hampton Court House, Middlesex.*

*Gothic seat at Painswick, Gloucestershire.*

inspiration from it. As we have seen, he spent a good deal of time in Gloucestershire and it is highly likely that he would have seen Goldney nearby.

This, then, completes our tour of rococo gardens and the identification of some of the strands. Rococo is a product of its time but is part of the development of the garden in broader terms and should be seen in the context of a pictorial approach to garden design, scene-making in a progressively naturalistic but also ornamental way. Rococo is a paradox, a tension between realism and extreme artifice, and could not survive for long. Even at its height it laid itself open to abuse and to the charge of bad taste, which the nineteenth century did not hesitate to level at it. Now, however, at a distance of more than two hundred years, the elements of charm and elusiveness (so much having disappeared) are more likely to hold sway and make us regret that we cannot now see what Thomas Robins and his fortunate contemporaries saw.

# Further reading

## General and background

Christie, Anthony. *Chinese and Goths*. 1987. (Duplicated booklet.)
Conner, Patrick. *Oriental Architecture in the West*. Thames and Hudson, 1979.
Desmond, Ray. *Bibliography of British Gardens*. St Paul's, 1984.
*The Garden*. New Perspectives, 1979.
Georgian Group. *Georgian Arcadia*. Georgian Group/Colnaghi, 1987.
Harris, John. *Sir William Chambers*. Zwemmer, 1970.
Hind, Charles (editor). *The Rococo in England: A Symposium*. Victoria and Albert Museum, 1986. This contains an article by John Harris on gardens: 'The Artinatural Style'.
Hunt, John Dixon. *William Kent: Landscape Garden Designer*. Zwemmer, 1987.
Jacques, David. *Georgian Gardens: The Reign of Nature*. Batsford, 1983 (paperback 1990).
Jones, Barbara. *Follies and Grottoes*. Constable, 1974.
Mott, George, and Aall, Sally. *Follies and Pavilions*. Pavilion, 1989.
*Oxford Companion to Gardens*. Oxford University Press, 1986.
Smith, Julia Abel. *Pavilions in Peril*. SAVE, 1987.
Snodin, Michael (editor). *Rococo: Art and Design in Hogarth's England*. Trefoil/Victoria and Albert Museum, 1984.
Sotheby's. *The Glory of the Garden*. Sotheby's, 1987.
Thacker, Christopher. *The History of Gardens*. Croom Helm, 1979 (reissued subsequently as paperback).

## Particular gardens or designers

Edelstein, T. J. *Vauxhall Gardens*. Yale Center for British Art, 1983.
Harris, Eileen (editor). *Thomas Wright's 'Arbours and Grottos'*. Scolar Press, 1979.
Harris, Eileen. 'So Rare, So Elegant', *Country Life*, 18th December 1986, 1956-9. (Hampton Court House grotto.)
Harris, John. *Gardens of Delight: The Rococo English Landscape of Thomas Robins the Elder*. Basilisk, 1978.
Hellyer, Arthur. 'Only One of its Kind', *Country Life*, 15th June 1989, 156-61. (Painswick.)
Hellyer, Arthur. 'Picturebook Garden', *Country Life*, 20th July 1989, 72-5. (Belcombe.)
Jackson-Stops, Gervase. 'Arcadia Under the Plough', *Country Life*, 9th February 1989, 82-7. (Halswell.)
Jones, A. E. *The Story of Carshalton House*. London Borough of Sutton, 1980.

Lambert, David, and Harding, Stewart. 'Thomas Wright at Stoke Park', *Garden History*, 17, 1 (1989), 68-82.
McCarthy, Michael. 'Thomas Wright's *Designs for Temples* and Related Drawings for Garden Buildings', *Journal of Garden History*, 1, 1 (1981), 55-66.
McCarthy, Michael. 'Thomas Wright's Designs for Gothic Garden Buildings', *Journal of Garden History*, 1, 3 (1981), 239-52.
Savage, Robert. 'Natural History of the Goldney Garden Grotto, Clifton, Bristol', *Garden History*, 17, 1 (1989), 1-40.
White, Roger, and Mowl, Tim. 'Thomas Robins at Painswick', *Journal of Garden History*, 4, 3 (1984), 163-74.

# Gardens to visit

*Belcombe Court*, Bradford-on-Avon, Wiltshire. Write to the Administrator for an appointment.

*Bowood House*, Calne, Wiltshire. Telephone: 0249 812102.

*Carshalton House*, Carshalton, Surrey. Write to the Sister Superior for an appointment.

*Farnborough Hall* (Warwickshire), near Banbury, Oxfordshire. National Trust. Write to the owner for an appointment.

*Goldney Grotto*, Clifton, Bristol. Write to the Warden, Clifton Hill Hall of Residence, University of Bristol, Clifton, Bristol, for an appointment.

*Hagley Hall* (Worcestershire), near Stourbridge, West Midlands. Telephone: 0562 882408.

*Hampton Court House*, Bushy Park, Hampton Court, Middlesex. Telephone Marble Hill House for an appointment: 081-892 5115.

*Honington Hall*, Shipston-on-Stour, Warwickshire. Telephone: 0608 61434.

*Nuneham Courtenay*, Oxfordshire. Telephone: 0867 38551.

*Painshill Park*, Portsmouth Road, Cobham, Surrey. Telephone: 0932 68113.

*Painswick Rococo Garden*, Painswick, Gloucestershire. Telephone: 0452 813204.

*Shugborough*, Stafford, Staffordshire. National Trust. Telephone: 0889 881388.

*Wimpole Hall*, near Cambridge. National Trust. Telephone: 0223 207257.

*Wroxton Abbey*, near Banbury, Oxfordshire. Telephone: 0295 73551.

# Index

*Page numbers in italic refer to illustrations.*